SONGS OF THE SIERRAS

by

Joaquin Miller

LITERATURE HOUSE / GREGG PRESS
Upper Saddle River, N. J.

Republished in 1970 by
LITERATURE HOUSE
an imprint of The Gregg Press
121 Pleasant Avenue
Upper Saddle River, N. J. 07458

Standard Book Number—8398-1260-4
Library of Congress Card—71-104528

Printed in United States of America

JOAQUIN MILLER

The life of Cincinnatus Heine Miller was so fantastic that, even when one discounts some of the events for which we have only his word as evidence, we are left with a series of wild adventures which make Jack London's existence appear banal by comparison. Miller was born in 1837 near Liberty, Indiana, the son of a Quaker farmer, who was also a schoolmaster, and Margaret DeWitt Miller. (Miller later changed his first name to Joaquin in honor of Joaquin Murrieta, a Mexican bandit whom he admired and had defended in a newspaper article.) The father was evidently not successful, or else was a wanderer by nature, for in 1852, after having lived in at least three Indiana towns, the family joined a wagon train on its way to Oregon. After a difficult journey, the Millers reached Eugene, Oregon, where the boy worked on a farm and picked up a little education at the primitive schools and by reading what books were available. In 1855, he and a friend ran away to the California gold fields, where he found no gold but, lacking adequate food, acquired scurvy.

The next few years were spent wandering up and down the Pacific Coast, where he lived for a time with the Digger Indians, marrying a squaw, and joining them in their horse-stealing expeditions. In 1859 he was captured and imprisoned, but escaped. He returned to Oregon, and attended the newly founded Columbia College in Eugene, leaving that institution in 1860. He then taught school, read for the law, and was accepted at the bar in 1861. Too restless to practice law, he abandoned the idea and went to Idaho to try to make his fortune in mining, but failed. With his partner Isaac Mossman, he founded a pony express route between the Washington Territory and Idaho, and with the profits from this enterprise went on to buy the *Democratic Register* in Eugene. The local authorities closed down his paper for being "pro-Confederate."

Meanwhile, Miller had written two volumes of poetry, which received no critical recognition. After a second marriage that quickly was dissolved, he went to Canyon City, Oregon, and was commissioned to lead an expedition against hostile Indians. As a reward for the successful completion of the dangerous mission, he was made judge of the Court of Grant County. 1870 found him in San Francisco in the company of Bret Harte, Warren Stoddard, and other literary figures. Appearing in London, he privately printed *Pacific Poems* and *Songs of the Sierras,* which were acclaimed in England but ignored by critics and the public in America, with the notable exception of Walt Whitman. In London Miller did everything possible to live up to the English image of the rough, democratic American frontiersman. He appeared in the upper-class literary salons attired like a circus performer in sombrero, cowboy boots, buckskins, and with either cigar or chewing tobacco stuck in his mouth, insulted the nobility and literati in salty frontier language. This "representative" American was a tremendous hit in Mayfair, and Miller soon was engaged to a rich, aristocratic debutante. Hailed by W. M. Rossetti, praised as the "Byron of Oregon," Miller played the role with gusto, but, as usual, became bored, and embarked on travels to Hawaii, South America, Continental Europe, the Near East, and back to the United States.

In 1883 he married Abbie Leland, and in 1886 the couple acquired an estate in the hills above Oakland, California. Here, Miller erected monuments to his boyhood hero, John C. Frémont, to Robert Browning, and to Moses, as well as a funeral pyre for his own use. He planted the seeds of eucalyptus trees, which are growing today. Miller left this curious home in 1897, to serve a New York paper as correspondent in the Klondike. In 1900, he witnessed the Boxer Rebellion in China. He died at his California home in 1913, and, as a final gesture, his ashes were scattered over the Sierras.

It was the achievement of this splendid, flamboyant man to celebrate in poetry and prose the freedom, beauty, and grandeur of the Old West. His phrases are too often rhetorical, but never lack sincerity or emotional power. If he was occasionally absurd in real life, it was with the knowledge that he was an actor who was expected to rise to the occasion when called upon to act like a "Westerner." He lived his works, and although the style of his verses cannot be compared with that of Whitman, they are also an affirmation of the sense of destiny which was felt by Americans, as they watched or participated in the westward expansion. The naive and courageous words of his poems "Columbus" and "Kit Carson's Ride" were, not many years ago, part of the patriotic education of millions of schoolchildren.

Upper Saddle River, N. J. F. C. S.
December, 1969

SONGS OF THE SIERRAS.

Songs of the Sierras.

BY

JOAQUIN MILLER.

BOSTON:
ROBERTS BROTHERS.
1871.

Entered according to Act of Congress, in the year 1871, by

C. H. MILLER,

In the Office of the Librarian of Congress at Washington.

CAMBRIDGE:
PRESS OF JOHN WILSON AND SON.

TO MAUD.

CONTENTS.

	PAGE
ARIZONIAN	1
WITH WALKER IN NICARAGUA	23
CALIFORNIAN	65
THE LAST TASCHASTAS	107
INA	129
THE TALE OF THE TALL ALCALDE	195
KIT CARSON'S RIDE	243
BURNS AND BYRON	255
MYRRH	267
EVEN SO	277

ARIZONIAN.

*Because the skies were blue, because
The sun in fringes of the sea
Was tangled, and delightfully
Kept dancing on as in a waltz,
And tropic trees bow'd to the seas,
And bloom'd and bore, years through and through,
And birds in blended gold and blue
Were thick and sweet as swarming bees,
And sang as if in paradise,
And all that paradise was spring —
Did I too sing with lifted eyes,
Because I could not choose but sing.*

*With garments full of sea-winds blown
From isles beyond of spice and balm,
Beside the sea, beneath her palm,
She waits as true as chisell'd stone.
My childhood's child! my June in May!
So wiser than thy father is,
These lines, these leaves, and all of this
Are thine, — a loose, uncouth bouquet.
So wait and watch for sail and sign;
A ship shall mount the hollow seas,
Blown to thy place of blossom'd trees,
And birds, and song, and summer-shine.*

*I throw a kiss across the sea,
I drink the winds as drinking wine,
And dream they all are blown from thee:
I catch the whisper'd kiss of thine.
Shall I return with lifted face,
Or head held down as in disgrace,
To hold thy two brown hands in mine?*

ENGLAND, 1871.

SONGS OF THE SIERRAS.

ARIZONIAN.

"And I have said, and I say it ever,
 As the years go on and the world goes over,
'Twere better to be content and clever
In tending of cattle and tossing of clover,
In the grazing of cattle and the growing of grain,
Than a strong man striving for fame or gain;
Be even as kine in the red-tipp'd clover;
For they lie down and their rests are rests,
And the days are theirs, come sun come rain,
To lie, rise up, and repose again;
While we wish, yearn, and do pray in vain,
And hope to ride on the billows of bosoms,
And hope to rest in the haven of breasts,
Till the heart is sicken'd and the fair hope dead;
Be even as clover with its crown of blossoms,
Even as blossoms ere the bloom is shed,

Kiss'd by kine and the brown sweet bee —
For these have the sun, and moon, and air,
And never a bit of the burthen of care;
And with all of our caring what more have we?
I would court content like a lover lonely,
I would woo her, win her, and wear her only,
And never go over this white sea wall
For gold or glory or for aught at all."

He said these things as he stood with the Squire
By the river's rim in the fields of clover,
While the stream flow'd under and the clouds flew over,
With the sun tangled in and the fringes afire.
So the Squire lean'd with a kind desire
To humor his guest, and to hear his story;
For his guest had gold, and he yet was clever,
And mild of manner; and, what was more, he,
In the morning's ramble, had praised the kine,
The clover's reach and the meadows fine,
And so made the Squire his friend for ever.

His brow was brown'd by the sun and weather,
And touch'd by the terrible hand of time;
His rich black beard had a fringe of rime,

As silk and silver inwove together.
There were hoops of gold all over his hands,
And across his breast, in chains and bands,
Broad and massive as belts of leather.
And the belts of gold were bright in the sun,
But brighter than gold his black eyes shone
From their sad face-setting so swarth and dun,
Brighter than beautiful Santan stone,
Brighter even than balls of fire,
As he said, hot-faced, in the face of the Squire: —

"The pines bow'd over, the stream bent under
The cabin cover'd with thatches of palm,
Down in a cañon so deep, the wonder
Was what it could know in its clime but calm.
Down in a cañon so cleft asunder
By sabre-stroke in the young world's prime,
It look'd as broken by bolts of thunder,
And bursted asunder and rent and riven
By earthquakes, driven, the turbulent time
A red cross lifted red hands to heaven.
And this in the land where the sun goes down,
And gold is gather'd by tide and by stream,
And maidens are brown as the cocoa brown,

And a life is a love and a love is a dream;
Where the winds come in from the far Cathay
With odor of spices and balm and bay,
And summer abideth for aye and aye,
Nor comes in a tour with the stately June,
And comes too late and returns too soon
To the land of the sun and of summer's noon.

"She stood in the shadows as the sun went down,
Fretting her curls with her fingers brown,
As tall as the silk-tipp'd tassel'd corn —
Stood strangely watching as I weigh'd the gold
We had wash'd that day where the river roll'd;
And her proud lip curl'd with a sun-clime scorn,
As she ask'd, 'Is she better or fairer than I? —
She, that blonde in the land beyond,
Where the sun is hid and the seas are high —
That you gather in gold as the years go on,
And hoard and hide it away for her
As a squirrel burrows the black pine-burr?'

"Now the gold weigh'd well, but was lighter of weight
Than we two had taken for days of late,
So I was fretted, and, brow a-frown,

I said, 'She is fairer, and I loved her first,
And shall love her last come the worst to worst.'
Now her eyes were black and her skin was brown,
But her lips grew livid and her eyes afire
As I said this thing . and higher and higher
The hot words ran, when the booming thunder
Peal'd in the crags and the pine-tops under,
While up by the cliff in the murky skies
It look'd as the clouds had caught the fire —
The flash and fire of her wonderful eyes.

" She turn'd from the door and down to the river,
And mirror'd her face in the whimsical tide ;
Then threw back her hair, as if throwing a quiver,
As an Indian throws it back far from his side
And free from his hands, swinging fast to the shoulder,
When rushing to battle ; and, rising, she sigh'd
And shook, and shiver'd as aspens shiver.
Then a great green snake slid into the river,
Glistening, green, and with eyes of fire ;
Quick, double-handed she seized a boulder,
And cast it with all the fury of passion,
As with lifted head it went curving across,
Swift darting its tongue like a fierce desire,

Curving and curving, lifting higher and higher,
Bent and beautiful as a river moss;
Then, smitten, it turn'd, bent, broken and doubled,
And lick'd, red-tongued, like a forkèd fire,
And sank, and the troubled waters bubbled,
And then swept on in their old swift fashion.

"I lay in my hammock: the air was heavy
And hot and threat'ning; the very heaven
Was holding its breath; and bees in a bevy
Hid under my thatch; and birds were driven
In clouds to the rocks in a hurried whirr
As I peer'd down by the path for her.
She stood like a bronze bent over the river,
The proud eyes fix'd, the passion unspoken —
When the heavens broke like a great dyke broken.
Then, ere I fairly had time to give her
A shout of warning, a rushing of wind
And the rolling of clouds and a deafening din
And a darkness that had been black to the blind
Came down, as I shouted, 'Come in! come in!
Come under the roof, come up from the river,
As up from a grave — come now, or come never!'
The tassel'd tops of the pines were as weeds,

The red-woods rock'd like to lake-side reeds,
And the world seem'd darken'd and drown'd for ever.

"One time in the night as the black wind shifted,
And a flash of lightning stretch'd over the stream,
I seem'd to see her with her brown hands lifted —
Only seem'd to see, as one sees in a dream —
With her eyes wide wild and her pale lips press'd,
And the blood from her brow and the flood to her breast;
When the flood caught her hair as the flax in a wheel,
And wheeling and whirling her round like a reel,
Laugh'd loud her despair, then leapt long like a steed,
Holding tight to her hair, folding fast to her heel,
Laughing fierce, leaping far as if spurr'd to its speed ..
Now mind, I tell you all this did but seem —
Was seen as you see fearful scenes in a dream;
For what the devil could the lightning show
In a night like that, I should like to know!

"And then I slept, and sleeping I dream'd
Of great green serpents with tongues of fire,
And of death by drowning, and of after death —
Of the day of judgment, wherein it seem'd

That she, the heathen, was bidden higher,
Higher than I; that I clung to her side,
And clinging struggled, and struggling cried,
And crying, waken'd, all weak of my breath.

"Long leaves of the sun lay over the floor,
And a chipmonk chirp'd in the open door,
But above on his crag the eagle scream'd,
Scream'd as he never had scream'd before.
I rush'd to the river: the flood had gone
Like a thief, with only his tracks upon
The weeds and grasses and warm wet sand;
And I ran after with reaching hand,
And call'd as I reach'd and reach'd as I ran,
And ran till I came to the cañon's van,
Where the waters lay in a bent lagoon,
Hook'd and crook'd like the hornèd moon.

"Here in the surge where the waters met,
And the warm wave lifted, and the winds did fret
The wave till it foam'd with rage on the land,
She lay with the wave on the warm white sand;
Her rich hair trail'd with the trailing weeds,
And her small brown hands lay prone or lifted

As the wave sang strophes in the broken reeds,
Or paused in pity, and in silence sifted
Sands of gold, as upon her grave.
And as sure as you see yon browsing kine,
And breathe the breath of your meadows fine,
When I went to my waist in the warm white wave
And stood all pale in the wave to my breast,
And reach'd for her in her rest and unrest,
Her hands were lifted and reach'd to mine.

"Now mind, I tell you I cried, 'Come in!
Come in to the house, come out from the hollow,
Come out of the storm, come up from the river!'
Cried, and call'd, in that desolate din,
Though I did not rush out, and in plain words give her
A wordy warning of the flood to follow,
Word by word, and letter by letter:
But she knew it as well as I, and better;
For once in the desert of New Mexico
When I sought frantically far and wide
For the famous spot where Apaches shot
With bullets of gold their buffalo,
And she followed faithfully at my side,
I threw me down in the hard hot sand

Utterly famish'd, and ready to die,
And a speck arose in the red-hot sky —
A speck no larger than a lady's hand —
While she at my side bent tenderly over,
Shielding my face from the sun as a cover,
And wetting my face, as she watch'd by my side,
From a skin she had borne till the high noon-tide,
(I had emptied mine in the heat of the morning)
When the thunder mutter'd far over the plain
Like a monster bound or a beast in pain,
She sprang the instant, and gave the warning,
With her brown hand pointed to the burning skies.
I was too weak unto death to arise,
And I pray'd for death in my deep despair,
And did curse and clutch in the sand in my rage,
And bite in the bitter white ashen sage,
That covers the desert like a coat of hair;
But she knew the peril, and her iron will,
With heart as true as the great North Star,
Did bear me up to the palm-tipp'd hill,
Where the fiercest beasts in a brotherhood,
Beasts that had fled from the plain and far,
In perfectest peace expectant stood,
With their heads held high, and their limbs a-quiver;

And ere she barely had time to breathe
The boiling waters began to seethe
From hill to hill in a booming river,
Beating and breaking from hill to hill —
Even while yet the sun shot fire,
Without the shield of a cloud above —
Filling the cañon as you would fill
A wine-cup, drinking in swift desire,
With the brim new-kiss'd by the lips you love.

"So you see she knew — knew perfectly well,
As well as I could shout and tell,
The mountains would send a flood to the plain,
Sweeping the gorge like a hurricane,
When the fire flash'd, and the thunder fell.
Therefore it is wrong, and I say therefore
Unfair, that a mystical brown wing'd moth
Or midnight bat should for evermore
Fan my face with its wings of air,
And follow me up, down, everywhere,
Flit past, pursue me, or fly before,
Dimly limning in each fair place
The full fix'd eyes and the sad brown face,
So forty times worse than if it were wroth.

"I gather'd the gold I had hid in the earth,
Hid over the door and hid under the hearth:
Hoarded and hid, as the world went over,
For the love of a blonde by a sun-brown'd lover;
And I said to myself, as I set my face
To the East and afar from the desolate place,
'She has braided her tresses, and through her tears
Look'd away to the West, for years, the years
That I have wrought where the sun tans brown;
She has waked by night, she has watch'd by day,
She has wept and wonder'd at my delay,
Alone and in tears, with her head held down,
Where the ships sail out and the seas swirl in,
Forgetting to knit and refusing to spin.
She shall lift her head, she shall see her lover,
She shall hear his voice like a sea that rushes,
She shall hold his gold in her hands of snow,
And down on his breast she shall hide her blushes,
And never a care shall her true heart know,
While the clods are below, or the clouds are above her.'

"On the fringe of the night she stood with her pitcher
At the old town-pump: and oh! passing fair.

'I am riper now,' I said, 'but am richer,'
And I lifted my hand to my beard and hair;
'I am burnt by the sun, I am brown'd by the sea;
I am white of my beard, and am bald, may be;
Yet for all such things what can her heart care?'
Then she moved; and I said, 'How marvellous fair!'
She look'd to the West, with her arm arch'd over;
'Looking for me, her sun-brown'd lover,'
I said to myself, with a hot heart-thump,
And stepp'd me nearer to the storm-stain'd pump,
As approaching a friend; for 'twas here of old
Our troths were plighted and the tale was told.

"How young she was and how fair she was!
How tall as a palm, and how pearly fair,
As the night came down on her glorious hair!
Then the night grew deep and the eye grew dim,
And a sad-faced figure began to swim
And float in my face, flit past, then pause,
With her hands held up and her head held down,
Yet face to face; and her face was brown.
Now why did she come and confront me there,
With the mould on her face and the moist in her hair,
And a mystical stare in her marvellous eyes?

I had call'd to her twice, 'Come in! come in!
Come out of the storm to the calm within!'
Now, that is the reason that I make complain
That for ever and ever her face should arise,
Facing face to face with her great sad eyes.
I said then to myself, and I say it again,
Gainsay it you, gainsay it who will,
I shall say it over and over still,
And will say it ever, for I know it true,
That I did all that a man could do
(Some good men's doings are done in vain)
To save that passionate child of the sun,
With her love as deep as the doubled main,
And as strong and fierce as a troubled sea —
That beautiful bronze with its soul of fire,
Its tropical love and its kingly ire —
That child as fix'd as a pyramid,
As tall as a tula and as pure as a nun —
And all there is of it the all I did,
As often happens, was done in vain.
So there is no bit of her blood on me.

"'She is marvellous young and is wonderful fair,'
I said again, and my heart grew bold,

And beat and beat a charge for my feet.
'Time that defaces us, places, and replaces us,
And trenches the faces as in furrows for tears,
Has traced here nothing in all these years.
'Tis the hair of gold that I vex'd of old,
The marvellous flowing flower of hair,
And the peaceful eyes in their sweet surprise
That I have kiss'd till the head swam round,
And the delicate curve of the dimpled chin,
And the pouting lips and the pearls within
Are the same, the same, but so young, so fair!'
My heart leapt out and back at a bound,
As a child that starts, then stops, then lingers.
'How wonderful young!' I lifted my fingers
And fell to counting the round years over
That I had dwelt where the sun goes down.
Four full hands, and a finger over!
'She does not know me, her truant lover,'
I said to myself, for her brow was a-frown
As I stepp'd still nearer, with my head held down,
All abash'd and in blushes my brown face over;
'She does not know me, her long-lost lover,
For my beard's so long and my skin's so brown,
That I well might pass myself for another.'

So I lifted my voice and I spoke aloud:
'Annette, my darling! Annette Macleod!'
She started, she stopp'd, she turn'd, amazed,
She stood all wonder with her eyes wild-wide,
Then turn'd in terror down the dusk wayside,
And cried as she fled, 'The man is crazed,
And calls the maiden name of my mother!'

" From a scene that saddens, from a ghost that wearies,
From a white isle set in a wall of seas,
From the kine and clover and all of these
I shall set my face for the fierce Sierras.
I shall make me mates on the stormy border,
I shall beard the grizzly, shall battle again,
And from mad disorder shall mould me order
And a wild repose for a weary brain.

" Let the world turn over, and over, and over,
And toss and tumble like a beast in pain,
Crack, quake, and tremble, and turn full over
And die, and never rise up again;
Let her dash her peaks through the purple cover,
Let her plash her seas in the face of the sun —
I have no one to love me now, not one,

In a world as full as a world can hold;
So I will get gold as I erst have done,
I will gather a coffin top-full of gold,
To take to the door of Death, to buy
Content, when I double my hands and die.
There is nothing that is, be it beast or human,
Love of maiden or the lust of man,
Curse of man or the kiss of woman,
For which I care or for which I can
Give a love for a love or a hate for a hate,
A curse for a curse or a kiss for a kiss,
Since life has neither a bane nor a bliss,
To one that is cheek by jowl with fate;
For I have lifted and reach'd far over
To the tree of promise, and have pluck'd of all
And ate — ate ashes, and myrrh, and gall.
Go down, go down to the fields of clover,
Down with the kine in the pastures fine,
And give no thought, or care, or labor
For maid or man, good name or neighbor;
For I have given, and what have I? —
Given all my youth, my years, and labor,
And a love as warm as the world is cold,
For a beautiful, bright, and delusive lie.

Gave youth, gave years, gave love for gold,
Giving and getting, yet what have I
But an empty palm and a face forgotten,
And a hope that's dead, and a heart that's rotten?
Red gold on the waters is no part bread,
But sinks dull-sodden like a lump of lead,
And returns no more in the face of Heaven.
So the dark day thickens at the hope deferr'd,
And the strong heart sickens and the soul is stirr'd
Like a weary sea when his hands are lifted,
Imploring peace, with his raiment drifted
And driven afar and rent and riven.

" The red ripe stars hang low overhead,
Let the good and the light of soul reach up,
Pluck gold as plucking a butter-cup:
But I am as lead and my hands are red;
There is nothing that is that can wake one passion
In soul or body, or one sense of pleasure,
No fame or fortune in the world's wide measure,
Or love full-bosomed or in any fashion.

" The doubled sea, and the troubled heaven,
Starr'd and barr'd by the bolts of fire,

In storms where stars are riven, and driven
As clouds through heaven, as a dust blown higher;
The angels hurl'd to the realms infernal,
Down from the walls in unholy wars,
That man misnameth the falling stars;
The purple robe of the proud Eternal,
The Tyrian blue with its fringe of gold,
Shrouding His countenance, fold on fold —
All are dull and tame as a tale that is told.
For the loves that hasten and the hates that linger,
The nights that darken and the days that glisten,
And men that lie and maidens that listen,
I care not even the snap of my finger.

"So the sun climbs up, and on, and over,
And the days go out and the tides come in,
And the pale moon rubs on the purple cover
Till worn as thin and as bright as tin;
But the ways are dark and the days are dreary,
And the dreams of youth are but dust in age,
And the heart gets harden'd, and the hands grow weary
Holding them up for their heritage.

"And the strain'd heart-strings wear bare and brittle,

And the fond hope dies when so long deferr'd;
Then the fair hope lies in the heart interr'd,
So stiff and cold in its coffin of lead.
For you promise so great and you gain so little;
For you promise so great of glory and gold,
And gain so little that the hands grow cold;
And for gold and glory you gain instead
A fond heart sicken'd and a fair hope dead.

"So I have said, and I say it over,
And can prove it over and over again,
That the four-footed beasts on the red-crown'd clover,
The pied and hornèd beasts on the plain
That lie down, rise up, and repose again,
And do never take care or toil or spin,
Nor buy, nor build, nor gather in gold,
Though the days go out and the tides come in,
Are better than we by a thousand fold;
For what is it all, in the words of fire,
But a vexing of soul and a vain desire?"

WITH WALKER IN NICARAGUA.

*Come to my sun land! Come with me
To the land I love; where the sun and sea
Are wed forever: where palm and pine
Are filled with singers; where tree and vine
Are voiced with prophets! O come, and you
Shall sing a song with the seas that swirl
And kiss their hands to the cold white girl,
To the maiden moon in her mantle of blue.*

WITH WALKER IN NICARAGUA.

I.

HE was a brick: let this be said
 Above my brave dishonored dead.
I ask no more, this is not much,
Yet I disdain a colder touch
To memory as dear as his;
For he was true as any star,
And brave as Yuba's grizzlies are,
Yet gentle as a panther is,
Mouthing her young in her first fierce kiss;
Tall, courtly, grand as any king,
Yet simple as a child at play,
In camp and court the same alway,
And never moved at any thing;
A dash of sadness in his air,
Born, may be, of his over care,
And, may be, born of a despair
In early love — I never knew;

I question'd not, as many do,
Of things as sacred as this is;
I only knew that he to me
Was all a father, friend, could be;
I sought to know no more than this
Of history of him or his.

A piercing eye, a princely air,
A presence like a chevalier,
Half angel and half Lucifer;
Fair fingers, jewell'd manifold
With great gems set in hoops of gold;
Sombréro black, with plume of snow
That swept his long silk locks below;
A red serape with bars of gold,
Heedless falling, fold on fold;
A sash of silk, where flashing swung
A sword as swift as serpent's tongue,
In sheath of silver chased in gold;
A face of blended pride and pain,
Of mingled pleading and disdain,
With shades of glory and of grief;
And Spanish spurs with bells of steel
That dash'd and dangl'd at the heel —

The famous filibuster chief
Stood by his tent 'mid tall brown trees
That top the fierce Cordilleras,
With brawn arm arch'd above his brow; —
Stood still — he stands, a picture, now —
Long gazing down the sunset seas.

II.

WHAT strange strong bearded men were these
He led toward the tropic seas!
Men sometime of uncommon birth,
Men rich in histories untold,
Who boasted not, though more than bold,
Blown from the four parts of the earth.
Men mighty-thew'd as Sampson was,
That had been kings in any cause,
A remnant of the races past;
Dark-brow'd as if in iron cast,
Broad-breasted as twin gates of brass, —
Men strangely brave and fiercely true,
Who dared the West when giants were,
Who err'd, yet bravely dared to err;
A remnant of that early few
Who held no crime or curse or vice

As dark as that of cowardice;
With blendings of the worst and best
Of faults and virtues that have blest
Or cursed or thrill'd the human breast.

They rode, a troop of bearded men,
Rode two and two out from the town,
And some were blonde and some were brown
And all as brave as Sioux; but when
From San Bennetto south the line
That bound them in the laws of men
Was passed, and peace stood mute behind
And streamed a banner to the wind
The world knew not, there was a sign
Of awe, of silence, rear and van.
Men thought who never thought before;
I heard the clang and clash of steel
From sword at hand or spur at heel
And iron feet, but nothing more.
Some thought of Texas, some of Maine,
But more of rugged Tennessee, —
Of scenes in Southern vales of wine,
And scenes in Northern hills of pine
As scenes they might not meet again;

IN NICARAGUA.

And one of Avon thought, and one
Thought of an isle beneath the sun,
And one of Rowley, one the Rhine,
And one turned sadly to the Spree.

  Defeat meant something more than death:
The world was ready, keen to smite,
As stern and still beneath its ban
With iron will and bated breath,
Their hands against their fellow-man,
They rode — each man an Ishmaelite.
But when we struck the hills of pine,
These men dismounted, doffed their cares,
Talked loud and laughed old love affairs,
And on the grass took meat and wine,
And never gave a thought again
To land or life that lay behind,
Or love, or care of any kind
Beyond the present cross or pain.

  And I, a waif of stormy seas,
A child among such men as these,
Was blown along this savage surf
And rested with them on the turf,

And took delight below the trees.
I did not question, did not care
To know the right or wrong. I saw
That savage freedom had a spell,
And loved it more than I can tell,
And snapped my fingers at the law.
I bear my burden of the shame, —
I shun it not, and naught forget,
However much I may regret:
I claim some candor to my name,
And courage cannot change or die. —
Did they deserve to die? they died.
Let justice then be satisfied,
And as for me, why what am I?

The standing side by side till death,
The dying for some wounded friend,
The faith that failed not to the end,
The strong endurance till the breath
And body took their ways apart,
I only know. I keep my trust.
Their vices! earth has them by heart.
Their virtues! they are with their dust.

How wound we through the solid wood,
With all its broad boughs hung in green,
With lichen-mosses trail'd between!
How waked the spotted beasts of prey,
Deep sleeping from the face of day,
And dash'd them like a troubled flood
Down some defile and denser wood!

And snakes, long, lithe and beautiful
As green and graceful-bough'd bamboo,
Did twist and twine them through and through
The boughs that hung red-fruited full.
One, monster-sized, above me hung,
Close eyed me with his bright pink eyes,
Then raised his folds, and sway'd and swung,
And lick'd like lightning his red tongue,
Then oped his wide mouth with surprise;
He writhed and curved, and raised and lower'd
His folds like liftings of the tide,
And sank so low I touched his side,
As I rode by, with my broad sword.

The trees shook hands high overhead,
And bow'd and intertwined across

The narrow way, while leaves and moss
And luscious fruit, gold-hued and red,
Through all the canopy of green,
Let not one sunshaft shoot between.

Birds hung and swung, green-robed and red,
Or droop'd in curved lines dreamily,
Rainbows reversed, from tree to tree,
Or sang low-hanging overhead —
Sang low, as if they sang and slept,
Sang faint, like some far waterfall,
And took no note of us at all,
Though nuts that in the way were spread
Did crush and crackle as we stept.

Wild lilies, tall as maidens are,
As sweet of breath, as pearly fair,
As fair as faith, as pure as truth,
Fell thick before our every tread,
As in a sacrifice to ruth,
And all the air with perfume fill'd
More sweet than ever man distill'd.
The ripen'd fruit a fragrance shed
And hung in hand-reach overhead,

In nest of blossoms on the shoot,
The bending shoot that bore the fruit.

How ran the monkeys through the leaves!
How rush'd they through, brown clad and blue,
Like shuttles hurried through and through
The threads a hasty weaver weaves!

How quick they cast us fruits of gold,
Then loosen'd hand and all foothold,
And hung limp, limber, as if dead,
Hung low and listless overhead;
And all the time, with half-oped eyes
Bent full on us in mute surprise —
Look'd wisely too, as wise hens do
That watch you with the head askew.

The long days through from blossom'd trees
There came the sweet song of sweet bees,
With chorus-tones of cockatoo
That slid his beak along the bough,
And walk'd and talk'd and hung and swung,
In crown of gold and coat of blue,
The wisest fool that ever sung,
Or had a crown, or held a tongue.

Oh when we broke the sombre wood
And pierced at last the sunny plain,
How wild and still with wonder stood
The proud mustangs with banner'd mane,
And necks that never knew a rein,
And nostrils lifted high, and blown,
Fierce breathing as a hurricane:
Yet by their leader held the while
In solid column, square, and file,
And ranks more martial than our own!

Some one above the common kind,
Some one to look to, lean upon,
I think is much a woman's mind;
But it was mine, and I had drawn
A rein beside the chief while we
Rode through the forest leisurely;
When he grew kind and questioned me
Of kindred, home, and home affair,
Of how I came to wander there,
And had my father herds and land
And men in hundreds at command?
At which I silent shook my head,
Then, timid, met his eyes and said,

"Not so. Where sunny-foot hills run
Down to the North Pacific sea,
And Willamette meets the sun
In many angles, patiently
My father tends his flocks of snow,
And turns alone the mellow sod
And sows some fields not over broad,
And mourns my long delay in vain,
Nor bids one serve-man come or go;
While mother from her wheel or churn,
And may be from the milking shed,
There lifts an humble weary head
To watch and wish for my return
Across the camas' blossom'd plain."

He held his bent head very low,
A sudden sadness in his air;
Then turned and touched my yellow hair
And took the long locks in his hand,
Toyed with them, smiled, and let them go,
Then thrummed about his saddle bow
As thought ran swift across his face;
Then turning sudden from his place,
He gave some short and quick command.

They brought the best steed of the band,
They swung a bright sword at my side,
He bade me mount and by him ride,
And from that hour to the end
I never felt the need of friend.

Far in the wildest quinine wood
We found a city old — so old,
Its very walls were turn'd to mould,
And stately trees upon them stood.
No history has mention'd it,
No map has given it a place;
The last dim trace of tribe and race —
The world's forgetfulnesss is fit.

It held one structure grand and moss'd,
Mighty as any castle sung,
And old when oldest Ind was young,
With threshold Christian never cross'd;
A temple builded to the sun,
Along whose sombre altar-stone
Brown bleeding virgins had been strown
Like leaves, when leaves are crisp and dun,

IN NICARAGUA.

In ages ere the Sphinx was born,
Or Babylon had birth or morn.

My chief led up the marble step —
He ever led, broad blade in hand —
When down the stones, with double hand
Clutch'd to his blade, a savage leapt,
Hot bent to barter life for life.
The chieftain drove his bowie knife
Full through his thick and broad breast-bone,
And broke the point against the stone,
The dark stone of the temple wall.
I saw him loose his hold and fall
Full length with head hung down the step;
I saw run down a ruddy flood
Of rushing pulsing human blood.
Then from the crowd a woman crept
And kiss'd the gory hands and face,
And smote herself. Then one by one
The dark crowd crept and did the same,
Then bore the dead man from the place.
Down darken'd aisles the brown priests came,
So picture-like, with sandall'd feet
And long gray dismal grass-wove gowns,

So like the pictures of old time,
And stood all still and dark of frowns,
At blood upon the stone and street.
So we laid ready hand to sword
And boldly spoke some bitter word;
But they were stubborn still, and stood
Dark frowning as a winter wood,
And mutt'ring something of the crime
Of blood upon the temple stone,
As if the first that it had known.

We turned toward the massive door
With clash of steel at heel, and with
Some swords all red and ready drawn.
I traced the sharp edge of my sword
Along the marble wall and floor
For crack or crevice; there was none.
From one vast mount of marble stone
The mighty temple had been cored
By nut-brown children of the sun;
When stars were newly bright and blithe
Of song along the rim of dawn,
A mighty marble monolith!

* * * * *

III.

* * * * *

THROUGH marches through the mazy wood,
And may be through too much of blood,
At last we came down to the seas.
A city stood, white-wall'd, and brown
With age, in nest of orange trees;
And this we won, and many a town
And rancho reaching up and down,
Then rested in the red-hot days
Beneath the blossom'd orange trees,
Made drowsy with the drum of bees,
And drank in peace the south-sea breeze,
Made sweet with sweeping boughs of bays.

Well! there were maidens, shy at first,
And then, ere long, not over shy,
Yet pure of soul and proudly chare.
No love on earth has such an eye!
No land there is is bless'd or curs'd
With such a limb or grace of face,
Or gracious form, or genial air!
In all the bleak North-land not one
Hath been so warm of soul to me

As coldest soul by that warm sea,
Beneath the bright hot centred sun.

No lands where any ices are
Approach, or ever dare compare
With warm loves born beneath the sun.
The one the cold white steady star,
The lifted shifting sun the one.
I grant you fond, I grant you fair,
I grant you honor, trust and truth,
And years as beautiful as youth,
And many years beyond the sun,
And faith as fix'd as any star;
But all the North-land hath not one
So warm of soul as sun-maids are.

I was but in my boyhood then,
I count my fingers over, so,
And find it years and years ago,
And I am scarcely yet of men.
But I was tall and lithe and fair,
With rippled tide of yellow hair,
And prone to mellowness of heart;
While she was tawny-red like wine,

With black hair boundless as the night.
As for the rest I knew my part,
At least was apt, and willing quite
To learn, to listen, and incline
To teacher warm and wise as mine.

O bright, bronzed maidens of the sun!
So fairer far to look upon
Than curtains of the Solomon,
Or Kedar's tents, or any one,
Or any thing beneath the sun!
What follow'd then? What has been done,
And said, and writ, and read, and sung?
What will be writ and read again,
While love is life, and life remain? —
While maids will heed, and men have tongue?

What follow'd then? But let that pass.
I hold one picture in my heart,
Hung curtain'd, and not any part
Of all its dark tint ever has
Been look'd upon by any one.
But if, may be, one brave and strong
As liftings of the bristled sea

Steps forth from out the days to be
And knocks heart-wise, and enters bold
A rugged heart inured to wrong —
As one would storm a strong stronghold —
Strong-footed, and most passing fair
Of truth, and thought beyond her years,
We two will lift the crape in tears,
Will turn the canvas to the sun,
Will trace the features one by one
Of my dear dead, in still despair.

Love well who will, love wise who can,
But love, be loved, for God is love;
Love pure, like cherubim above;
Love maids, and hate not any man.
Sit as sat we by orange tree,
Beneath the broad bough and grape-vine
Top-tangled in the tropic shine,
Close face to face, close to the sea,
And full of the red-centred sun,
With grand sea-songs upon the soul,
Roll'd melody on melody,
Like echoes of deep organ's roll,
And love, nor question any one.

IN NICARAGUA.

If God is love, is love not God?
As high priests say, let prophets sing,
Without reproach or reckoning;
This much I say, knees knit to sod,
And low voice lifted, questioning.

Let eyes be not dark eyes, but dreams,
Or drifting clouds with flashing fires,
Or far delights, or fierce desires,
Yet not be more than well beseems;
Let hearts be pure and strong and true,
Let lips be luscious and blood-red,
Let earth in gold be garmented
And tented in her tent of blue,
Let goodly rivers glide between
Their leaning willow walls of green,
Let all things be fill'd of the sun,
And full of warm winds of the sea,
And I beneath my vine and tree
Take rest, nor war with any one;
Then I will thank God with full cause,
Say this is well, is as it was.

Let lips be red, for God has said

Love is like one gold-garmented,
And made them so for such a time.
Therefore let lips be red, therefore
Let love be ripe in ruddy prime,
Let hope beat high, let hearts be true,
And you be wise thereat, and you
Drink deep, and ask not any more.

Let red lips lift, proud curl'd, to kiss,
And round limbs lean and raise and reach
In love too passionate for speech,
Too full of blessedness and bliss
For any thing but this and this;
Let luscious lips lean hot to kiss
And swoon in love, while all the air
Is redolent with balm of trees,
And mellow with the song of bees,
While birds sit singing everywhere —
And you will have not any more
Than I in boyhood, by that shore
Of olives, had in years of yore.

Let the unclean think things unclean;
I swear tip-toed, with lifted hands,

That we were pure as sea-washed sands,
That not one coarse thought came between;
Believe or disbelieve who will,
Unto the pure all things are pure;
As for the rest, I can endure
Alike their good will or their ill.

She boasted Montezuma's blood,
Was pure of soul as Tahoe's flood,
And strangely fair and princely soul'd,
And she was rich in blood and gold —
More rich in love grown over-bold
From its own consciousness of strength.
How warm! Oh, not for any cause
Could I declare how warm she was,
In her brown beauty and hair's length.
We loved in the sufficient sun,
We lived in elements of fire,
For love is fire and fierce desire;
Yet lived as pure as priest and nun.

We lay slow rocking in the bay
In birch canoe beneath the crags
Thick, topp'd with palm, like sweeping flags

Between us and the burning day.
The red-eyed crocodile lay low
Or lifted from his rich rank fern,
And watch'd us and the tide by turn,
And we slow cradled to and fro.

And slow we cradled on till night,
And told the old tale, overtold,
As misers in recounting gold
Each time do take a new delight.
With her pure passion-given grace
She drew her warm self close to me;
And, her two brown hands on my knee,
And her two black eyes in my face,
She then grew sad and guess'd at ill,
And in the future seem'd to see
With woman's ken of prophecy;
Yet proffer'd her devotion still.
And plaintive so, she gave a sign,
A token cut of virgin gold,
That all her tribe should ever hold
Its wearer as some one divine,
Nor touch him with a hostile hand.
And I in turn gave her a blade,

A dagger, worn as well by maid
As man, in that half-lawless land;
It had a massive silver hilt,
Had a most keen and cunning blade,
A gift by chief and comrades made
For reckless blood at Rivas spilt.
"Show this," said I, "too well 'tis known,
And worth an hundred lifted spears,
Should ill beset your sunny years;
There is not one in Walker's band,
But at the sight of this alone,
Will reach a brave and ready hand,
And make your right or wrong his own."

IV.

*   *   *   *   *

Love while 'tis day; night cometh soon,
Wherein no man or maiden may;
Love in the strong young prime of day;
Drink drunk with love in ripe red noon,
Red noon of love and life and sun;
Walk in love's light as in sunshine,
Drink in that sun as drinking wine,

Drink swift, nor question any one;
For loves change sure as man or moon,
And wane like warm full days of June.

O Love, so fair of promises,
Bend here thy brow, blow here thy kiss,
Bend here thy bow above the storm
But once, if only this once more.
Comes there no patient Christ to save,
Touch and re-animate thy form
Long three days dead and in the grave?
Spread here thy silken net of jet;
Since man is false, since maids forget,
Since man must fall for his sharp sin,
Be thou the pit that I fall in;
I seek no safer fall than this.
Since man must die for some dark sin,
Blind leading blind, let come to this,
And my death-crime be one deep kiss.
Lo! I have found another land,
May I not find another love,
True, trusting as a bosom'd dove,
To lay its whole heart in my hand?
But lips that leap and cling and crush,

And limbs that twist and intertwine
With passion as a passion-vine,
And veins that throb and swell and rush —
Be ye forbidden fruit and wine.
Such passion is not fair or fit
Or fashion'd tall — touch none of it.

  *   *   *   *   *
  *   *   *   *   *

Ill comes disguised in many forms:
Fair winds are but a prophecy
Of foulest winds full soon to be —
The brighter these, the blacker they;
The clearest night has darkest day,
And brightest days bring blackest storms.
There came reverses to our arms;
I saw the signal-light's alarms
At night red-crescenting the bay.
The foe pour'd down a flood next day
As strong as tides when tides are high,
And drove us bleeding in the sea,
In such wild haste of flight that we
Had hardly time to arm and fly.

Blown from the shore, borne far a-sea,

I lifted my two hands on high
With wild soul plashing to the sky,
And cried, "O more than crowns to me
Farewell at last to love and thee!"
I walk'd the deck, I kiss'd my hand
Back to the far and fading shore,
And bent a knee as to implore,
Until the last dark head of land
Slid down behind the dimpled sea.
At last I sank in troubled sleep,
A very child, rock'd by the deep,
Sad questioning the fate of her
Before the savage conqueror.

The loss of comrades, power, place,
A city wall'd, cool shaded ways,
Cost me no care at all; somehow
I only saw her sad brown face,
And — I was younger then than now.

Red flash'd the sun across the deck,
Slow flapp'd the idle sails, and slow
The black ship cradled to and fro.
Afar my city lay, a speck

IN NICARAGUA. 51

Of white against a line of blue;
Around, half lounging on the deck,
Some comrades chatted two by two.
I held a new-fill'd glass of wine,
And with the mate talk'd as in play
Of fierce events of yesterday,
To coax his light life into mine.

He jerk'd the wheel, as slow he said,
Low laughing with averted head,
And so, half sad: "You bet they'll fight;
They follow'd in canim, canoe,
A perfect fleet, that on the blue
Lay dancing till the mid of night.
Would you believe! one little cuss —
(He turn'd his stout head slow sidewise,
And 'neath his hat-rim took the skies) —
"In petticoats did follow us
The livelong night, and at the dawn
Her boat lay rocking in the lee,
Scarce one short pistol-shot from me."
This said the mate, half mournfully,
Then peck'd at us; for he had drawn,
By bright light heart and homely wit,

A knot of us around the wheel,
Which he stood whirling like a reel,
For the still ship reck'd not of it.

" And where's she now ? " one careless said,
With eyes slow lifting to the brine,
Swift swept the instant far by mine ;
The bronzed mate listed, shook his head,
Spirted a stream of amber wide
Across and over the ship side,
Jerk'd at the wheel, and slow replied :

" She had a dagger in her hand,
She rose, she raised it, tried to stand,
But fell, and so upset herself ;
Yet still the poor brown savage elf,
Each time the long light wave would toss
And lift her form from out the sea,
Would shake a strange bright blade at me,
With rich hilt chased a cunning cross.
At last she sank, but still the same
She shook her dagger in the air,
As if to still defy and dare,
And sinking seem'd to call your name."

IN NICARAGUA.

I dash'd my wine against the wall,
I rush'd across the deck, and all
The sea I swept and swept again,
With lifted hand, with eye and glass,
But all was idle and in vain.
I saw a red-bill'd sea-gull pass,
A petrel sweeping round and round,
I heard the far white sea-surf sound,
But no sign could I hear or see
Of one so more than seas to me.

I cursed the ship, the shore, the sea,
The brave brown mate, the bearded men;
I had a fever then, and then
Ship, shore and sea were one to me;
And weeks we on the dead waves lay,
And I more truly dead than they.
At last some rested on an isle;
The few strong-breasted with a smile
Returning to the sunny shore,
Scarce counting of the pain or cost,
Scarce recking if they won or lost;
They sought but action, ask'd no more;
They counted life but as a game,

With full per cent against them, and
Staked all upon a single hand,
And lost or won, content the same.

I never saw my chief again,
I never sought again the shore,
Or saw my white-wall'd city more.
I could not bear the more than pain
At sight of blossom'd orange trees
Or blended song of birds and bees,
The sweeping shadows of the palm
Or spicy breath of bay and balm.
And, striving to forget the while,
I wander'd through the dreary isle,
Here black with juniper, and there
Made white with goats in summer coats,
The only things that anywhere
We found with life in all the land,
Save birds that ran long-bill'd and brown,
Long-legg'd and still as shadows are,
Like dancing shadows, up and down
The sea-rim on the swelt'ring sand.

The warm sea laid his dimpled face,

With every white hair smoothed in place,
As if asleep against the land;
Great turtles slept upon his breast,
As thick as eggs in any nest;
I could have touched them with my hand.

* * * * *
* * * * *

I would some things were dead and hid,
Well dead and buried deep as hell,
With recollection dead as well,
And resurrection God-forbid.
They irk me with their weary spell
Of fascination, eye to eye,
And hot mesmeric serpent hiss,
Through all the dull eternal days.
Let them turn by, go on their ways,
Let them depart or let me die;
For life is but a beggar's lie,
And as for death, I grin at it;
I do not care one whiff or whit
Whether it be or that or this.

I give my hand; the world is wide;
Then farewell memories of yore,

Between us let strife be no more;
Turn as you choose to either side;
Say, Fare-you-well, shake hands and say —
Speak loud, and say with stately grace,
Hand clutching hand, face bent to face —
Farewell for ever and a day.

O passion-toss'd and bleeding past,
Part now, part well, part wide apart,
As ever ships on ocean slid
Down, down the sea, hull, sail, and mast;
And in the album of my heart
Let hide the pictures of your face,
With other pictures in their place,
Slid over like a coffin's lid.

* * * * *
* * * * *

The days and grass grow long together;
They now fell short and crisp again,
And all the fair face of the main
Grew dark and wrinkled at the weather.
Through all the summer sun's decline
Fell news of triumphs and defeats,

IN NICARAGUA. 57

Of hard advances, hot retreats —
Then days and days and not a line.

At last one night they came. I knew
Ere yet the boat had touch'd the land
That all was lost: they were so few
I near could count them on one hand;
But he the leader led no more.
The proud chief still disdain'd to fly,
But, like one wreck'd, clung to the shore,
And struggled on, and struggling fell
From power to a prison-cell,
And only left that cell to die.

* * * * *

My recollection, like a ghost,
Goes from this sea to that sea-side,
Goes and returns as turns the tide,
Then turns again unto the coast.
I know not which I mourn the most,
My brother or my virgin bride,
My chief or my unwedded wife.
The one was as the lordly sun,
To joy in, bask in, and admire;

The peaceful moon was as the one,
To love, to look to, and desire;
And both a part of my young life.

* * * * *

Years after, shelter'd from the sun
Beneath a Sacramento bay,
A black Muchacho by me lay
Along the long grass crisp and dun,
His brown mule browsing by his side,
And told with all a Peon's pride
How he once fought, how long and well,
Broad breast to breast, red hand to hand,
Against a foe for his fair land,
And how the fierce invader fell;
And artless told me how he died.

To die with hand and brow unbound
He gave his gems and jewell'd sword;
Thus at the last the warrior found
Some freedom for his steel's reward.
He walk'd out from the prison-wall
Dress'd like a prince for a parade,
And made no note of man or maid,

IN NICARAGUA.

But gazed out calmly over all;
Then look'd afar, half paused, and then
Above the mottled sea of men
He kiss'd his thin hand to the sun;
Then smiled so proudly none had known
But he was stepping to a throne,
Yet took no note of any one.
A nude brown beggar Peon child,
Encouraged as the captive smiled,
Look'd up, half scared, half pitying;
He stoop'd, he caught it from the sands,
Put bright coins in its two brown hands,
Then strode on like another king.

Two deep, a musket's length, they stood,
A-front, in sandals, nude, and dun
As death and darkness wove in one,
Their thick lips thirsting for his blood.
He took their black hands one by one,
And, smiling with a patient grace,
Forgave them all and took his place.
He bared his broad brow to the sun,
Gave one long last look to the sky,
The white-wing'd clouds that hurried by,

WITH WALKER

The olive hills in orange hue;
A last list to the cockatoo
That hung by beak from cocoa-bough
Hard by, and hung and sung as though
He never was to sing again,
Hung all red-crown'd and robed in green,
With belts of gold and blue between. —

A bow, a touch of heart, a pall
Of purple smoke, a crash, a thud,
A warrior's raiment rent, and blood,
A face in dust and — that was all.

Success had made him more than king;
Defeat made him the vilest thing
In name, contempt or hate can bring:
So much the leaded dice of war
Do make or mar of character.

Speak ill who will of him, he died
In all disgrace; say of the dead
His heart was black, his hands were red —
Say this much, and be satisfied;
Gloat over it all undenied.

I only say that he to me,
Whatever he to others was,
Was truer far than any one
That I have known beneath the sun,
Sinner, saint, or Pharisee,
As boy or man, for any cause;
I simply say he was my friend
When strong of hand and fair of fame:
Dead and disgraced, I stand the same
To him, and so shall to the end.

I lay this crude wreath on his dust,
Inwove with sad, sweet memories
Recall'd here by these colder seas.
I leave the wild bird with his trust,
To sing and say him nothing wrong;
I wake no rivalry of song.

He lies low in the levell'd sand,
Unshelter'd from the tropic sun,
And now of all he knew not one
Will speak him fair in that far land.
Perhaps 'twas this that made me seek,
Disguised, his grave one winter-tide;

A weakness for the weaker side,
A siding with the helpless weak.

A palm not far held out a hand,
Hard by a long green bamboo swung,
And bent like some great bow unstrung,
And quiver'd like a willow wand;
Beneath a broad banana's leaf,
Perch'd on its fruits that crooked hang,
A bird in rainbow splendor sang
A low sad song of temper'd grief.

No sod, no sign, no cross nor stone,
But at his side a cactus green
Upheld its lances long and keen;
It stood in hot red sands alone,
Flat-palm'd and fierce with lifted spears;
One bloom of crimson crown'd its head,
A drop of blood, so bright, so red,
Yet redolent as roses' tears.
In my left hand I held a shell,
All rosy lipp'd and pearly red;
I laid it by his lowly bed,
For he did love so passing well

IN NICARAGUA.

The grand songs of the solemn sea.
O shell! sing well, wild, with a will,
When storms blow loud and birds be still,
The wildest sea-song known to thee!

I said some things, with folded hands,
Soft whisper'd in the dim sea-sound,
And eyes held humbly to the ground,
And frail knees sunken in the sands.
He had done more than this for me,
And yet I could not well do more:
I turned me down the olive shore,
And set a sad face to the sea.

London, 1871.

CALIFORNIAN.

Glintings of day in the darkness,
Flashings of flint and of steel,
Blended in gossamer texture
The ideal and the real,
Limn'd like the phantom-ship shadow,
Crowding up under the keel.

CALIFORNIAN.

I.

I STAND beside the mobile sea;
   And sails are spread, and sails are furl'd
From farthest corners of the world,
And fold like white wings wearily.
Steamships go up, and some go down
In haste, like traders in a town,
And seem to see and beckon all.
Afar at sea some white shapes flee,
With arms stretch'd like a ghost's to me,
And cloud-like sails far blown and curl'd,
Then glide down to the under-world.
As if blown bare in winter blasts
Of leaf and limb, tall naked masts
Are rising from the restless sea,
So still and desolate and tall,
I seem to see them gleam and shine
With clinging drops of dripping brine.

Broad still brown wings flit here and there,
Thin sea-blue wings wheel everywhere,
And white wings whistle through the air:
I hear a thousand sea-gulls call.

Behold the ocean on the beach
Kneel lowly down as if in prayer.
I hear a moan as of despair,
While far at sea do toss and reach
Some things so like white pleading hands.
The ocean's thin and hoary hair
Is trail'd along the silver'd sands,
At every sigh and sounding moan.
'Tis not a place for mirthfulness,
But meditation deep, and prayer,
And kneelings on the salted sod,
Where man must own his littleness
And know the mightiness of God.
The very birds shriek in distress
And sound the ocean's monotone.

Dared I but say a prophecy,
As sang the holy men of old,
Of rock-built cities yet to be

CALIFORNIAN.

Along these shining shores of gold,
Crowding athirst into the sea,
What wondrous marvels might be told!
Enough, to know that empire here
Shall burn her loftiest, brightest star;
Here art and eloquence shall reign,
As o'er the wolf-rear'd realm of old;
Here learn'd and famous from afar,
To pay their noble court, shall come,
And shall not seek or see in vain,
But look on all with wonder dumb.

Afar the bright Sierras lie
A swaying line of snowy white,
A fringe of heaven hung in sight
Against the blue base of the sky.

I look along each gaping gorge,
I hear a thousand sounding strokes
Like giants rending giant oaks,
Or brawny Vulcan at his forge;
I see pick-axes flash and shine
And great wheels whirling in a mine.
Here winds a thick and yellow thread,

A moss'd and silver stream instead;
And trout that leap'd its rippled tide
Have turn'd upon their sides and died.

Lo! when the last pick in the mine
Is rusting red with idleness,
And rot yon cabins in the mould,
And wheels no more croak in distress,
And tall pines reassert command,
Sweet bards along this sunset shore
Their mellow melodies will pour;
Will charm as charmers very wise,
Will strike the harp with master hand,.
Will sound unto the vaulted skies
The valor of these men of old —
The mighty men of 'Forty-nine;
Will sweetly sing and proudly say,
Long, long agone there was a day
When there were giants in the land.

II.

CURAMBO! what a cloud of dust
Comes dashing down like driven gust!

And who rides rushing on the sight
Adown yon rocky long defile,
Swift as an eagle in his flight,
Fierce as a winter's storm at night
Blown from the bleak Sierra's height,
Careering down some yawning gorge?
His face is flush'd, his eye is wild,
And 'neath his courser's sounding feet
(A glance could barely be more fleet)
The rocks are flashing like a forge.
Such reckless rider! — I do ween
No mortal man his like has seen.
And yet, but for his long serape
All flowing loose, and black as crape,
And long silk locks of blackest hair
All streaming wildly in the breeze,
You might believe him in a chair,
Or chatting at some country fair
With friend or señorita rare,
He rides so grandly at his ease.

But now he grasps a tighter rein,
A red rein wrought in golden chain,
And in his tapidaros stands,

Half turns and shakes two bloody hands,
And shouts defiance at his foe;
Now lifts his broad hat from his brow
As if to challenge fate, and now
His hand drops to his saddle-bow
And clutches something gleaming there
As if to something more than dare,
While halts the foe that follow'd fast
As rushing wave or raving blast,
More sudden-swift than though were prest
All bridle-bands at one behest.

The stray winds lift the raven curls,
Soft as a fair Castilian girl's,
And press a brow so full and high
Its every feature does belie
The thought he is compell'd to fly;
A brow as open as the sky
On which you gaze and gaze again
As on a picture you have seen
And often sought to see in vain,
That seems to hold a tale of woe
Or wonder, that you fain would know;
A brow cut deep as with a knife,

With many a dubious deed in life;
A brow of blended pride and pain,
And yearnings for what should have been.

He grasps his gilded gory rein,
And wheeling like a hurricane,
Defying wood, or stone, or flood,
Is dashing down the gorge again.
Oh never yet has prouder steed
Borne master nobler in his need!
There is a glory in his eye
That seems to dare and to defy
Pursuit, or time, or space, or race.
His body is the type of speed,
While from his nostril to his heel
Are muscles as if made of steel.
He is not black, nor gray, nor white,
But 'neath that broad serape of night
And locks of darkness streaming o'er,
His sleek sides seem a fiery red —
They may be red with gushing gore.

What crimes have made that red hand red?
What wrongs have written that young face

With lines of thought so out of place?
Where flies he? And from whence has fled?
And what his lineage and race?
What glitters in his heavy belt,
And from his furr'd catenas gleam?
What on his bosom that doth seem
A diamond bright or dagger's hilt?
The iron hoofs that still resound
Like thunder from the yielding ground
Alone reply; and now the plain,
Quick as you breathe and gaze again,
Is won, and all pursuit is vain.

III.

I STAND upon a stony rim,
Stone-paved and pattern'd as a street;
A rock-lipp'd cañon plunging south,
As if it were earth's open'd mouth,
Yawns deep and darkling at my feet;
So deep, so distant, and so dim
Its waters wind, a yellow thread,
And call so faintly and so far,
I turn aside my swooning head.

I feel a fierce impulse to leap
Adown the beetling precipice,
Like some lone, lost, uncertain star;
To plunge into a place unknown,
And win a world all, all my own;
Or if I might not meet that bliss,
At least escape the curse of this.

  I gaze again. A gleaming star
Shines back as from some mossy well
Reflected from blue fields afar.
Brown hawks are wheeling here and there,
And up and down the broken wall
Cling clumps of dark green chaparral,
While from the rent rocks, gray and bare,
Blue junipers hang in the air.

  Here, cedars sweep the stream, and here,
Among the boulders moss'd and brown
That time and storms have toppled down
From towers undefiled by man,
Low cabins nestle as in fear,
And look no taller than a span.
From low and shapeless chimneys rise

Some tall straight columns of blue smoke,
And weld them to the bluer skies;
While sounding down the sombre gorge
I hear the steady pick-axe stroke,
As if upon a flashing forge.

Another scene, another sound!—
Sharp shots are fretting through the air,
Red knives are flashing everywhere,
And here and there the yellow flood
Is purpled with warm smoking blood.
The brown hawk swoops low to the ground,
And nimble chip-monks, small and still,
Dart stripèd lines across the sill
That lordly feet shall press no more.
The flume lies warping in the sun,
The pan sits empty by the door,
The pick-axe on its bed-rock floor
Lies rusting in the silent mine.
There comes no single sound nor sign
Of life, beside yon monks in brown
That dart their dim shapes up and down
The rocks that swelter in the sun;
But dashing round yon rocky spur

Where scarce a hawk would dare to whirr,
Fly horsemen reckless in their flight.
One wears a flowing black capote,
While down the cape doth flow and float
Long locks of hair as dark as night,
And hands are red that erst were white.

All up and down the land to-day
Black desolation and despair
It seems have sat and settled there,
With none to frighten them away.
Like sentries watching by the way
Black chimneys topple in the air,
And seem to say, Go back, beware!
While up around the mountain's rim
Are clouds of smoke, so still and grim
They look as they are fasten'd there.

A lonely stillness, so like death,
So touches, terrifies all things,
That even rooks that fly o'erhead
Are hush'd, and seem to hold their breath,
To fly with muffled wings,
And heavy as if made of lead.

Some skulls that crumble to the touch,
Some joints of thin and chalk-like bone,
A tall black chimney, all alone,
That leans as if upon a crutch,
Alone are left to mark or tell,
Instead of cross or cryptic stone,
Where fair maids loved or brave men fell.

* * * * *

I look along the valley's edge,
Where swings the white road like a swell
Of surf, along a sea of hedge
And black and brittle chaparral,
And enters like an iron wedge
Drove in the mountain dun and brown,
As if to split the hills in twain.
Two clouds of dust roll o'er the plain,
And men ride up and men ride down,
And hot men halt, and curse and shout,
And coming coursers plunge and neigh.
The clouds of dust are roll'd in one —
And horses, horsemen, where are they?
Lo! through a rift of dust and dun,
Of desolation and of rout,

I see some long white daggers flash,
I hear the sharp hot pistols crash,
And curses loud in mad despair
Are blended with a plaintive prayer
That struggles through the dust and air.

The cloud is lifting like a veil:
The frantic curse, the plaintive wail
Have died away; nor sound nor word
Along the dusty plain is heard
Save sounding of yon courser's feet,
Who flies so fearfully and fleet,
With gory girth and broken rein,
Across the hot and trackless plain.
Behold him, as he trembling flies,
Look back with red and bursting eyes
To where his gory master lies.
The cloud is lifting like a veil,
But underneath its drifting sail
I see a loose and black capote
In careless heed far fly and float,
So vulture-like above a steed
Of perfect mould and passing speed.

Here lies a man of giant mould,
His mighty right arm, perfect bare
Save but its sable coat of hair,
Is clutching in its iron clasp
A clump of sage, as if to hold
The earth from slipping from his grasp;
While, stealing from his brow, a stain
Of purple blood and gory brain
Yields to the parch'd lips of the plain,
Swift to resolve to dust again.

Lo! friend and foe blend here and there
With dusty lips and trailing hair:
Some with a cold and sullen stare,
Some with their red hands clasp'd in prayer.

Here lies a youth, whose fair face is
Still holy from a mother's kiss,
With brow as white as alabaster,
Save a tell-tale powder-stain
Of a deed and a disaster
That will never come again,
With their perils and their pain.

The tinkle of bells on the bended hills.

The hum of bees in the orange trees,
And the lowly call of the beaded rills
Are heard in the land as I look again
Over the peaceful battle-plain.
Murderous man from the field has fled,
Fled in fear from the face of his dead.
He battled, he bled, he ruled a day —
And peaceful Nature resumes her sway.
And the sward where yonder corses lie,
When the verdant season shall come again,
Shall greener grow than it grew before;
Shall again in sun-clime glory vie
With the gayest green in the tropic scene,
Taking its freshness back once more
From them that despoil'd it yesterday.

IV.

The sun is red and flush'd and dry,
And fretted from his weary beat
Across the hot and desert sky,
And swollen as from overheat,
And failing too; for see, he sinks
Swift as a ball of burnish'd ore:

It may be fancy, but methinks
He never fell so fast before.

 I hear the neighing of hot steeds,
I see the marshalling of men
That silent move among the trees
As busily as swarming bees
With step and stealthiness profound,
On carpetings of spindled weeds,
Without a syllable or sound
Save clashing of their burnish'd arms,
Clinking dull death-like alarms —
Grim bearded men and brawny men
That grope among the ghostly trees.
Were ever silent men as these?
Was ever sombre forest deep
And dark as this? Here one might sleep
While all the weary years went round,
Nor wake nor weep for sun or sound.

 A stone's-throw to the right, a rock
Has rear'd his head among the stars —
An island in the upper deep —
And on his front a thousand scars

Of thunder's crash and earthquake's shock
Are seam'd as if by sabre's sweep
Of gods, enraged that he should rear
His front amid their realms of air.

What moves along his beetling brow,
So small, so indistinct and far,
This side yon blazing evening star,
Seen through that redwood's shifting bough?
A lookout on the world below?
A watcher for the friend — or foe?
This still troop's sentry it must be,
Yet seems no taller than my knee.

But for the grandeur of this gloom,
And for the chafing steeds' alarms,
And brown men's sullen clash of arms,
This were but as a living tomb.
These weeds are spindled, pale and white,
As if nor sunshine, life nor light
Had ever reach'd this forest's heart.
Above, the redwood boughs entwine
As dense as copse of tangled vine —
Above, so fearfully afar,

It seems as 'twere a lesser sky,
A sky without a moon or star,
The moss'd boughs are so thick and high.
At every lisp of leaf I start!
Would I could hear a cricket trill,
Or that yon sentry from his hill
Might shout or show some sign of life,
The place does seem so deathly still.
"Mount ye, and forward for the strife!"
Who by yon dark trunk sullen stands,
With black serape and bloody hands,
And coldly gives his brief commands?

   They mount — away! Quick on his heel
He turns, and grasps his gleaming steel —
Then sadly smiles, and stoops to kiss
An upturn'd face so sweetly fair,
So sadly, saintly, purely fair,
So rich of blessedness and bliss!
I know she is not flesh and blood,
But some sweet spirit of this wood;
I know it by her wealth of hair,
And step on the unyielding air;
Her seamless robe of shining white,

Her soul-deep eyes of darkest night:
But over all and more than all
That could be said or can befall,
That tongue can tell or pen can trace,
That wondrous witchery of face.

Between the trees I see him stride
To where a red steed fretting stands
Impatient for his lord's commands:
And she glides noiseless at his side.

Lo! not a bud, or leaf, or stem,
Beneath her feet is bowed or bent;
They only nod, as if in sleep,
And all their grace and freshness keep;
And now will in their beauty bloom,
In pink and pearl habiliment,
As though fresh risen from a tomb,
For fairest sun has shone on them.

"The world is mantling black again!
Beneath us, o'er the sleeping plain,
Dull steel-gray clouds slide up and down
As if the still earth wore a frown.
The west is red with sunlight slain!"

(One hand toys with her waving hair,
Soft lifting from her shoulders bare;
The other holds the loosen'd rein,
And rests upon the swelling mane
That curls the curved neck o'er and o'er,
Like waves that swirl along the shore.
He hears the last retreating sound
Of iron on volcanic stone,
That echoes far from peak to plain,
And 'neath the dense wood's sable zone
He peers the dark Sierras down.)
" But darker yet shall be the frown,
And redder yet shall be the flame.
And yet I would that this were not —
That all, forgiven or forgot
Of curses deep and awful crimes,
Of blood and terror, could but seem
Some troubled and unholy dream;
That even now I could awake,
And waking find me once again
With hand and heart without a stain,
Swift gliding o'er that sunny lake,
Begirt with town and castle-wall,
Where first I saw the silver light —

CALIFORNIAN.   87

Begirt with blossoms, and the bloom
Of orange, sweet with the perfume
Of cactus, pomegranate, and all
The thousand sweets of tropic climes;
And, waking, see the mellow moon
Pour'd out in gorgeous plenilune
On silver ripples of that tide;
And, waking, hear soft music pour
Along that flora-formèd shore;
And, waking, find you at my side,
My father's moss'd and massive halls,
My brothers in their strength and pride."

(His hand forsakes her raven hair,
His eyes have an unearthly glare:
She shrinks and shudders at his side,
Then lifts to his her moisten'd eye,
And only looks her sad reply.
A sullenness his soul enthrals,
A silence born of hate and pride;
His fierce volcanic heart so deep
Is stirr'd, his teeth, despite his will,
Do chatter as if in a chill;

His very dagger at his side
Does shake and rattle in its sheath,
As blades of brown grass in a gale
Do rustle on the frosted heath :
And yet he does not bend or weep.)

"I did not vow a girlish vow,
Nor idle imprecation now
Will I bestow by boasting word —
Feats of the tongue become the knave.
A wailing in the land is heard
For those that will not come again;
And weeping for the rashly brave,
Who sleep in many a gulch and glen,
Has wet a hundred hearths with tears,
And darken'd them for years and years.
Would I could turn their tears to gore,
Make every hearth as cold as one
Is now upon that sweet lake shore,
Where my dear kindred dwelt of yore;
Where now is but an ashen heap,
And mass of mossy earth and stone;
Where round an altar black wolves keep
Their carnival and doleful moan;

Where hornèd lizards dart and climb,
And mollusks slide and leave their slime.

"But tremble not. This night, my own,
Shall see my fierce foe overthrown;
And ere the day-star gleams again
My horse's hoofs shall spurn the dead —
The still warm reeking dead of those
Who brought us all our bitter woes;
While all my glad returning way
Shall be as light as living day,
From ranchos, campos, burning red.
And then! And then, my peri pearl" —
(As if to charm her from her fears
And drive away the starting tears,
Again his small hand seeks a curl,
And voice forgets its sullen ire,
And eye forsakes its flashing fire) —
"Away to where the orange tree
Is white through all the cycled years,
And love lives an eternity;
Where birds are never out of tune
And life knows no decline of noon;
Where winds are sweet as woman's breath,

And purpled, dreamy, mellow skies
Are lovely as a woman's eyes, —
There, we in 'calm and perfect bliss
Of boundless faith and sweet delight
Shall realize the world above,
Forgetting all the wrongs of this,
Forgetting all of blood and death,
And all your terrors of to-night,
In pure devotion and deep love."

As gently as a mother bows
Her first-born sleeping babe above,
The cherish'd cherub lips to kiss
In her full blessedness and bliss,
He bends to her with stately air,
His proud head in its cloud of hair.
I do not heed the hallow'd kiss;
I do not hear the hurried vows
Of passion, faith, unfailing love;
I do not mark the prison'd sigh,
I do not meet the moisten'd eye:
A low sweet melody is heard
Like cooing of some Balize bird,
So fine it does not touch the air,

So faint it stirs not anywhere;
Faint as the falling of the dew,
Low as a pure unutter'd prayer,
The meeting, mingling, as it were,
Of souls in paradisal bliss.

Erect, again he grasps the rein
So tight, as to the seat he springs,
I see his red steed plunge and poise
And beat the air with iron feet,
And curve his noble glossy neck,
And toss on high his swelling mane,
And leap — away! he spurns the rein,
And flies so fearfully and fleet,
But for the hot hoofs' ringing noise
'Twould seem as if he were on wings.

And she is gone! Gone like a breath,
Gone like a white sail seen at night
A moment, and then lost to sight;
Gone like a star you look upon,
That glimmers to a bead, a speck,
Then softly melts into the dawn,
And all is still and dark as death.

V.

* * * * *

I look far down a dewy vale,
Where cool palms lean along a brook
As crooked as a shepherd's crook.
Red parrots call from orange trees,
Where white lips kiss the idle breeze,
And murmur with the hum of bees:
The gray dove coos his low love-tale.

With cross outstretch'd like pleading hands
That mutely plead the faith of Christ,
Amid the palms a low church stands:
I would that man might learn from these
The priceless victories of Peace,
And woo her 'mid these olive trees,
And win an earthly paradise.

I see black clouds of troops afar
Sweep like a surge that sweeps the shore,
And check'ring all the green hills o'er
Are battlements and signs of war.

I hear the hoarse-voiced cannon roar:
The red-mouth'd orators of war
Plead as they never plead before;
While outdone thunder stops his car
And leans in wonderment afar.

A fragment from the struggle rent
Forsakes the rugged battlement,
And winds it painfully and slow
Across the rent and riven lands
To where a gray church open stands,
As if it bore a load of woe.

Curambo! 'tis a chief they bear!
And by his black and flowing hair
Methinks I have seen him before.
A gray priest guides them through the door,
They lay him bleeding on the floor.

He moves, he lifts his feeble hand,
And points with tried and trenchèd brand,
And bids them to the battle-plain.
They turn — they pause: he bids again;
They turn a last time to their chief,

And gaze in silence and deep pain,
For silence speaks the deepest grief.
They clutch their blades; they turn — are gone:
And priest and chief are left alone.

"So here my last day has its close,
And here it ends. Here all is not.
I am content. 'Tis what I sought —
Revenge — and then my last repose.
Oh for the rest — for the rest eternal!
Oh for the deep and the dreamless sleep!
Where never a hope lures to deceive;
Where never a heart beats but to grieve;
Nor thoughts of heaven or hells infernal
Shall ever wake or dare to break
The rest of an everlasting sleep!

"Is there truth in the life eternal?
Will our memories never die?
Shall we relive in realms supernal
Life's resplendent and glorious lie?
Death has not one shape so frightful
But defiantly I would brave it;
Earth has nothing so delightful

But my soul would scorn to crave it,
Could I know for sure, for certain,
That the falling of the curtain
And the folding of the hands
Is the full and the final casting
Of accounts for the everlasting!
Everlasting, and everlasting!

" Well, I have known, I know not why,
Through all my dubious days of strife,
That when we live our deeds we die;
That man may in one hour live
All that his life can bear or give.
This I have done, and do not grieve,
For I am older by a score
Than many born long, long before,
If sorrows be the sum of life.

" Ay, I am old — old as the years
Could brand me with their blood and tears;
For with my fingers I can trace
Grief's trenches on my hollow face,
And through my thin frame I can feel
The pulses of my frozen heart

Beat with a dull uncertain start:
And, mirror'd in my sword, to-day,
Before its edge of gleaming steel
Had lost its lustre in the fray,
I saw around my temples stray
Thin straggling locks of steely gray.

"Fly, fly you, to yon snowy height,
And tell to her I fail, I die!
Fly swiftly, priest, I bid you!—fly
Before the falling of the night!
What! know her not? O priest, beware!
I warn you answer thus no more,
But bend your dull ear to the floor,
And hear you who she is, and where.

"She is the last, last of a line,
With blood as rich and warm as wine,
And blended blood of god and king;
Last of the Montezumas' line
Who dwelt up in the yellow sun,
And, sorrowing for man's despair,
Slid by his trailing yellow hair
To earth, to rule with love and bring

The blessedness of peace to us.
She is the last, last earthly one
Of all the children of the sun;
A sweet perfume still lingering
In essence pure, and living thus
In blessedness about the spot,
When rose, and bush, and bloom are not.

"Beside Tezcuco's flowery shore,
Where waves were washing evermore
The massive columns of its wall,
Stood Montezuma's mighty hall.
And here the Montezumas reign'd
In perfect peace and love unfeign'd,
Until, from underneath the sea
Where all sin is, or ought to be,
Came men of death and strange device,
Who taught a mad and mystic faith
Of crucifixion and of Christ,
More hated than the plague or death.

"Nay, do not swing your cross o'er me;
You cross'd you once, but do not twice,
Nor dare repeat the name of Christ;

Nor start, nor think to fly, nor frown,
While you the stole and surplice wear;
For I do clutch your sable gown,
And you shall hear my curse, or prayer,
And be my priest in my despair;
Since neither priest, nor sign, nor shrine
Is left in all the land, of mine.

"Enough! We know, alas! too well,
How red Christ ruled — Tonatiu fell.
The black wolf in our ancient halls
Unfrighten'd sleeps the live-long day.
The stout roots burst the mossy walls,
And in the moonlight wild dogs play
Around the plazas overgrown,
Where rude boars hold their carnivals.
The moss is on our altar-stone,
The mould on Montezuma's throne,
And symbols in the desert strown.

"And when your persecutions ceased
From troop, and king, and cowlèd priest,
That we had felt for centuries —
(Ah! know you, priest, that cross of thine

Is but death's symbol, and the sign
Of blood and butchery and tears?) —
And when return'd the faithful few,
Beside Tezcuco's sacred shore,
To build their broken shrines anew,
They number'd scarce a broken score.
Here dwelt my father — here *she* dwelt
Here kept one altar burning bright,
Last of the thousands that had shone
Along the mountain's brows of stone,
Last of a thousand stars of night.
To Tonatiu Ytzaqual we bow'd —
Nay, do not start, nor shape the sign
Of horror at this creed of mine,
Nor call again the name of Christ:
You cross you once, you cross you twice —
I warn you do not cross you thrice;
Nor will I brook a sign or look
Of anger at her faith avow'd.
I am no creedist. Faith to me
Is but a name for mystery.
I only know this faith is her's:
I care to know no more, to be
The truest of its worshippers.

"The Cold-men came across the plain
With gory blade and brand of flame:
I know not that they knew or cared
What was our race, or creed, or name;
I only know the Northmen dared
Assault and sack, for sake of gain
Of sacred vessels wrought in gold,
The temple where gods dwelt of old;
And that my father, brothers, dared
Defend their shrines — and all were slain.

"'Fly with the maid,' my father cried,
When first the fierce assault was made —
'A boat chafes at the causeway side,'
And in the instant was obey'd.
We gain'd the boat, sprang in, away
We dash'd along the dimpled tide.

"It must have been they thought we bore
The treasure in our flight and haste,
For in an instant from the shore
An hundred crafts were making chase,
And as their sharp prows drew apace

I caught a carbine to my face.
She, rising, dash'd it quick aside;
And, when their hands were stretch'd to clasp
The boat's prow in their eager grasp,
She turn'd to me and sudden cried,
'Come, come!' and plunged into the tide.
I plunged into the dimpled wave:
I had no thought but 'twas my grave;
But faith had never follower
More true than I to follow her.

"On, on through purple wave she cleaves,
As shoots a sunbeam through the leaves.
At last — what miracle was there! —
Again we breathed the welcome air;
And, resting by the rising tide,
The secret outlet of the lake,
Safe hid by trackless fern and brake,
With yellow lilies at her side,
She told me how in ages gone
Her Fathers built with sacred stone
This secret way beneath the tide,
That now was known to her alone.

"When night came on and all was still,
And stole the white moon down the hill
As soft, as if she too fear'd ill,
Again I sought the sacred halls
And on the curving causeway stood.
I look'd — naught but the blacken'd walls
And charr'd bones of my kindred blood
Was left beside the dimpled flood.

* * * * *
* * * * *

"Enough! Mine was no temper'd steel
To-day upon the stormy field,
As many trench'd heads yonder feel,
And many felt, that feel no more,
That fought beneath your cross and shield,
And, falling, called in vain to Christ.
You curs'd monk! dare you cross you thrice,
When I have warn'd you twice before?
To you and your damn'd faith I owe
My heritage of crime and woe;
You shall not live to mock me more
If there be temper in this brand,
Or nerve left in this bloody hand.

I start, I leave the stony ground,
Despite of blood or mortal wound,
Or darkness that has dimm'd the eye,
Or senses that do dance and reel —
I clutch a throat — I clench a steel —
I thrust — I fail — I fall — I die . . ."

VI.

She stands upon the wild watch-tower
And with her own hand feeds the flame —
The beacon-light to guide again
His coming from the battle-plain.
'Tis wearing past the midnight hour,
The latest that he ever came,
Yet silence reigns around the tower.

'Tis hours past the midnight hour:
She calls, she looks, she lists in vain
For sight or sound from peak or plain.
She moves along the beetling tower,
She leans, she lists forlorn and lone,
She stoops her ear low to the ground,

In hope to catch the welcome sound
Of iron on the rugged stone.

In vain she peers down in the night
But for one feeble flash of light
From flinty stone and feet of steel.
She stands upon the fearful rim,
Where even coolest head would reel,
And fearless leans her form far o'er
Its edge, and lifts her hands to him,
And calls in words as sweetly wild
As bleeding saint or sorrowing child.
She looks, she lists, she leans in vain,
In vain his dalliance does deplore;
She turns her to the light again,
And bids the watchman to the plain,
Defying night or dubious way,
To guide the flight or join the fray.

The day-star dances on the snow
That gleams along Sierra's crown
In gorgeous everlasting glow
And frozen glory and renown.
Yet still she feeds the beacon flame,
And lists, and looks, and leans in vain.

The day has dawn'd. She still is there!
Yet in her sad and silent air
I read the stillness of despair.
Why burns the red light on the tower
So brightly at this useless hour?
But see! The day-king hurls a dart
At darkness, and his cold black heart
Is pierced; and now, compell'd to flee,
Flies bleeding to the farther sea.
And now, behold, she radiant stands,
And lifts her thin white jewell'd hands
Unto the broad, unfolding sun,
And hails him Tonatiu and King
With hallow'd mien and holy prayer.
Her fingers o'er some symbols run,
Her knees are bow'd in worshipping
Her God, beheld when thine is not,
In form of faith long, long forgot.

Again she lifts her brown arms bare,
Far flashing in their bands of gold
And precious stones, rare, rich, and old.
Was ever mortal half so fair?
Was ever such a wealth of hair?

Was ever such a plaintive air?
Was ever such a sweet despair?

Still humbler now her form she bends;
Still higher now the flame ascends:
She bares her bosom to the sun.
Again her jewell'd fingers run
In signs and sacred form and prayer.
She bows with awe and holy air
In lowly worship to the sun;
Then rising calls her lover's name,
And leaps into the leaping flame.

I do not hear the faintest moan,
Or sound, or syllable, or tone.
The red flames stoop a moment down,
As if to raise her from the ground;
They whirl, they swirl, they sweep around
With light'ning feet and fiery crown;
Then stand up, tall, tip-toed, as one
Would hand a soul up to the sun.

THE LAST TASCHASTAS.

*The hills were brown, the heavens were blue,
A woodpecker pounded a pine-top shell,
While a partridge whistled the whole day through
For a rabbit to dance in the chapparal,
And a gray grouse drumm'd, "All's well, all's well."*

THE LAST TASCHASTAS.

PART FIRST.

WRINKLED and brown as a bag of leather,
    A squaw sits moaning long and low.
Yesterday she was a wife and mother,
To-day she is rocking her to and fro,
A childless widow, in weeds and woe.

An Indian sits in a rocky cavern
Whetting a flint in an arrow head;
His children are moving as still as shadows,
His squaw is moulding some balls of lead,
With her round face painted the battle-red.

An Indian sits in a black-jack jungle,
Where a grizzly bear has rear'd her young,
Whetting a flint on a granite boulder,
And his quiver is over his brown back hung,
And his face is streak'd and his bow is strung.

THE LAST TASCHASTAS.

An Indian hangs from a cliff of granite,
Like an eagle's nest built in the air,
Looking away to the east, and watching
The smoke of the cabins curling there,
And eagles' feathers are in his hair.

In belt of wampum, in battle fashion,
An Indian watches with wild desire.
He is red with paint, he is black with passion,
And grand as a god in his savage ire,
As he leans and listens till stars are a-fire.

Sombre and sullen and sad, the chieftain
Looks from the mountain far into the sea.
Just before him beat in the white billows,
Just behind him the toppled tall tree
And chopping of woodmen, knee buckl'd to knee.

Long he looks, and he leans and listens —
Waves before him, behind him white waves
Beating and breaking on the last Taschastas;
Waves that have toppled across red braves,
Levell'd, and left not a sign of their graves.

"Awake and arise! O, remnant Taschastas!
Awake to the life that is death in the land,
And this shall be doubled in dust contented"—
He lifts to heaven his doubled right hand,
Flashing afar with a great gold band.

PART SECOND.
* * * * *

ALL together, all in council,
In a cañon wall'd so high
That no thing could ever reach them
Save some stars dropp'd from the sky,
And the brown bats sweeping by:

Some were gray and thin and wiry,
Wise as brief, and brief as bold;
Some were young and fierce and fiery,
Some were stately tall, and told
Counsellings like kings of old.

Flamed the council-fire brighter,
Flash'd black eyes like diamond beads,
When a woman told her sorrows,
While a warrior told his deeds,
And a widow tore her weeds.

Then was lit the pipe of council
That their fathers smoked of old,
With its stem of manzinnetta,
And its bowl of quartz and gold,
And traditions manifold.

Lo! from lip to lip in silence
Burn'd it round the circle red,
Like an evil star slow passing
(Sign of battles and blood shed)
Round the heavens overhead.

Then the silence deep was broken
By the thunder rolling far,
As gods muttering in anger,
Or the bloody battle-car
Of a Christian king at war.

"'Tis the spirits of my Fathers
Mutt'ring vengeance in the skies;
And the flashing of the lightning
Is the anger of their eyes,
Bidding us in battle rise,"

THE LAST TASCHASTAS.

Cried the war-chief, now uprising,
Naked all above the waist,
While a belt of shells and silver
Held his tamoos to its place,
And the war-paint streak'd his face.

Women melted from the council,
Boys crept backward out of sight,
Till alone a wall of warriors
In their paint and battle-plight
Sat reflecting back the light.

"O my Fathers in the storm-cloud!" —
(Red arms tossing to the skies,
While the massive walls of granite
Seem'd to shrink to half their size,
And to mutter strange replies) —

"Soon we come, O angry Fathers,
Down the darkness you have cross'd :
Speak for hunting-grounds there for us ;
Those you left us we have lost —
Gone like blossoms in a frost.

"Warriors!" (and his arms fell folded
On his tawny swelling breast,
While his voice, now low and plaintive
As the waves in their unrest,
Touching tenderness confess'd,)

"Where is Wrotto, wise of counsel,
Yesterday here in his place?
A brave lies dead down in the valley,
Last brave of his line and race,
And a Ghost sits on his face.

"Where the boy the tender-hearted,
With his mother yestermorn?
Lo! a wigwam-door is darken'd,
And a mother mourns forlorn,
With her long locks toss'd and torn.

"Once like pines around a mountain
Did my braves in council stand;
Now I call you loud like thunder,
And you come at my command
Faint and few, with feeble hand.

THE LAST TASCHASTAS.

"Lo! our daughters have been gather'd
From among us by the foe,
Like the lilies they once gather'd
In the spring-time all aglow
From the banks of living snow.

"Through the land where we for ages
Laid the bravest, dearest dead,
Grinds the savage white-man's ploughshare,
Grinding sires' bones for bread —
We shall give them blood instead.

"I saw white skulls in a furrow,
And around the cursèd share
Clung the flesh of my own children;
And my mother's tangled hair
Trail'd along the furrow there.

"O my mother up in cloud-land!"
(Long arms lifting like the spray)
"Whet the flint heads in my arrows,
Make my heart as hard as they,
Nerve me like a bear at bay!

"Warriors! braves! I cry for vengeance!
And the dim ghosts of the dead
Unavenged do wail and shiver
In the storm-cloud overhead,
And shoot arrows battle-red."

Then he ceased, and sat among them,
With his long locks backward strown;
They as mute as men of marble,
He a king upon a throne,
And as still as polish'd stone.

Hard by stood the war-chief's daughter,
Taller than the tassel'd corn,
Sweeter than the kiss of morning,
Sad as some sweet star of morn,
Half defiant, half forlorn.

Robed in skins of stripèd panther
Lifting loosely to the air,
With a face a shade of sorrow,
And black eyes that said, Beware!
Nestled in a storm of hair;

THE LAST TASCHASTAS.

With her stripèd robes around her,
Fasten'd by an eagle's beak,
Stood she by the stately chieftain,
Proud and pure as Shasta's peak,
As she ventured thus to speak:

"Must the tomahawk of battle
Be unburied where it lies,
O, last war-chief of Taschastas?
Must the smoke of battle rise
Like a storm-cloud in the skies?

"True, some wretch has laid a brother
With his swift feet to the sun,
But because one bough is broken,
Must the broad oak be undone?
All the red-wood fell'd as one?

"True, the braves have faded, wasted
Like ripe blossoms in the rain,
But when we have spent the arrows,
Do we twang the string in vain,
And then snap the bow in twain?"

THE LAST TASCHASTAS.

Like a vessel in a tempest
Shook the warrior, wild and grim,
As he gazed out in the midnight,
As to things that beckon'd him,
And his eyes were moist and dim.

Then he turned, and to his bosom
Battle scarred, and strong as brass,
Tenderly the warrior press'd her
As if she were made of glass,
Murmuring, "Alas! alas!

"Loua Ellah! Spotted Lily!
Streaks of blood shall be the sign,
On their curs'd and mystic pages,
Representing me and mine!
By Tonatiu's fiery shrine!

"When the grass shall grow untrodden
In my war-path, and the plough
Shall be grinding through this cañon
Where my braves are gather'd now,
Still shall they record this vow.

"War and vengeance! rise, my warriors,
Rise and shout the battle-sign,
Ye who love revenge and glory!
Ye for peace, in silence, pine,
And no more be braves of mine."

Then the war-yell roll'd and echo'd
As they started from the ground,
Till an eagle from his cedar
Starting answered back the sound,
And flew circling round and round.

"Enough, enough, my kingly father!"
And the glory of her eyes
Flash'd the valor and the passion
That may sleep but never dies,
As she proudly thus replies:

"Shall the red-wood be a willow,
Pliant and as little worth?
It shall stand the king of forests,
Or its fall shall shake the earth,
Desolating heart and hearth!"

  *   *   *   *   *
  *   *   *   *   *

Part Third.

* * * * *

From cold east shore to warm west sea
The red men follow'd the red sun,
And, faint and failing fast as he,
Felt, sure as his, their race was run.
This ancient tribe, press'd to the wave,
There fain had slept a patient slave,
And died out as red embers die
From flames that once leapt hot and high;
But, roused to anger, half arose
Around that chief, a sudden flood,
At hot and hungry cry for blood;
Half drowsy shook a feeble hand,
Then sank back in a tame repose,
And left him to his fate and foes,
A stately wreck upon the strand.

His was no common mould of mind,
But made for action, ill or good.
Cast in another land and scene,
His restless, reckless will had been
A curse or blessing to his kind.

His eye was like the lightning's wing,
His voice was like a rushing flood;
He boasted Montezuma's blood,
And when a captive bound he stood
His presence look'd the perfect king.

'Twas held at first that he should die:
I never knew the reason why
A milder counsel did prevail,
Save that we shrank from blood, and save
That brave men do respect the brave.
Down sea sometimes there was a sail,
And far at sea, they said, an isle,
And he was sentenced to exile,
In open boat upon the sea
To go the instant on the main,
And never under penalty
Of death, to touch the shore again.
A troop of bearded buckskinn'd men
Bore him hard-hurried to the wave,
Placed him swift in the boat; and when
Swift pushing to the bristled sea,
His daughter rush'd down suddenly,
Threw him his bow, leapt from the shore

Into the boat beside the brave,
And sat her down and seized the oar,
And never question'd, made replies,
Or moved her lips, or raised her eyes.

His breast was like a gate of brass,
His brow was like a gather'd storm;
There is no chisell'd stone that has
So stately and complete a form,
In sinew, arm, and every part,
In all the galleries of art.

Gray, bronzed, and naked to the waist,
He stood half halting in the prow,
With quiver bare and idle bow.
His daughter sat with her sad face
Bent on the wave, with her two hands
Held tightly to the dripping oar;
And as she sat her dimpled knee
Bent lithe as wand of willow tree,
So round and full, so rich and free,
That no one would have ever known
That it had either joint or bone.

THE LAST TASCHASTAS. 123

The warm sea fondled with the shore,
And laid his white face on the sands.

  Her eyes were black, her face was brown,
Her breasts were bare, and there fell down
Such wealth of hair, it almost hid
The two, in its rich jetty fold—
Which I had sometime fain forbid,
They were so richer, fuller far
Than any polish'd bronzes are,
And richer hued than any gold.
On her brown arms and her brown hands
Were hoops of gold and golden bands,
Rough hammer'd from the virgin ore,
So heavy, they could hold no more.

  I wonder now, I wonder'd then,
That men who fear'd not gods nor men
Laid no rude hand at all on her.
I think she had a dagger slid
Down in her silver'd wampum belt;
It might have been, instead of hilt,
A flashing diamond hurry-hid
That I beheld — I could not know

For certain, we did hasten so;
And I know now less sure than then.
Deeds strangle memories of deeds,
Red blossoms wither, choked with weeds,
And floods drown memories of men.
Some things have happen'd since — and then
This happen'd years and years ago.

"Go, go!" the captain cried, and smote
With sword and boot the swaying boat,
Until it quiver'd as at sea
And brought the old chief to his knee.
He turn'd his face, and turning rose
With hand raised fiercely to his foes:
"Yes, we will go, last of my race,
Push'd by the robbers ruthlessly
Into the hollows of the sea,
From this the last, last resting-place.
Traditions of my Fathers say
A feeble few reach'd for the land,
And we reach'd them a welcome hand,
Of old, upon another shore;
Now they are strong, we weak as they,
And they have driven us before

Their faces, from that sea to this:
Then marvel not if we have sped
Sometime an arrow as we fled,
So keener than a serpent's kiss."

He turn'd a time unto the sun
That lay half hidden in the sea,
As in his hollows rock'd asleep,
All trembled and breathed heavily;
Then arch'd his arm, as you have done,
For sharp masts piercing through the deep.
No shore or tall ship met the eye,
Or isle, or sail, or any thing,
Save white sea-gulls on dripping wing,
And mobile sea and molten sky.

"Farewell! — push seaward, child!" he cried;
And quick the paddle-strokes replied.
Like lightning from the panther-skin
That bound his loins round about
He snatch'd a poison'd arrow out,
That like a snake lay hid within,
And twanged his bow. The captain fell
Prone on his face, and such a yell

Of triumph from that savage rose
As man may never hear again.
He stood as standing on the main,
The topmost main, in proud repose,
And shook his clench'd fist at his foes,
And called, and cursed them every one.
He heeded not the shouts and shot
That follow'd him, but grand and grim
Stood up against the level sun;
And, standing so, seem'd in his ire
So grander than a leaping fire.

And when the sun had left the sea,
That laves Abrep, and Blanco laves,
And left the land to death and me,
The only thing that I could see
Was, ever as the light boat lay
High lifted on the white-back'd waves,
A head as gray and tossed as they.

We raised the dead, and from his hands
Pick'd out the shells clutch'd as he lay,

And two by two bore him away,
And wiped his lips of blood and sands.
We bent and scoop'd a shallow home,
And laid him warm-wet in his blood,
Just as the lifted tide a-flood
Came charging in with mouth a-foam:
And as we turn'd, the sensate thing
Reach'd up, lick'd out its foamy tongue,
Lick'd out its tongue and tasted blood;
The white lips to the red earth clung
An instant, and then loosening
All hold just like a living thing,
Drew back sad-voiced and shuddering,
All stain'd with blood, a stripèd flood.

INA.

*Sad song of the wind in the mountains,
And the sea-wave of grass on the plain,
That breaks in bloom-foam by the fountains,
And forests that breaketh again
On the mountains, as breaketh a main.*

*Bold thoughts that were strong as the grizzlies,
But now weak in their prison of words;
Bright fancies that flash'd like the glaciers,
Now dimm'd like the lustre of birds,
And butterflies huddled as herds.*

*Sad symphony, wild, and unmeasured,
Weed warp, and woof woven in strouds,
Strange truths that a stray soul has treasured,
Truths seen as through folding of shrouds,
Or as stars through the rolling of clouds.*

INA.

Scene I.

A Hacienda near Tezcuco, Mexico.   Young Don Carlos
alone, looking out on the moonlit mountains.

Don Carlos.

POPOCATAPETL looms lone like an island
    Above the white cloud-waves that break up
        against him;
Around him white buttes in the moonlight are flashing
Like silver tents pitch'd in the fields of heaven;
While standing in line, in their snows everlasting,
Flash peaks, as my eyes into heaven are lifted,
Like milestones that lead to the city eternal.

Ofttime when the sun and the sea lay together,
Red-welded as one, in their red bed of lovers,
Embracing and blushing like loves newly wedded,
I have trod on the trailing crape fringes of twilight,
And stood there and listen'd, and lean'd with lips
    parted,

Till lordly peaks wrapp'd them, as chill night blew
over,
In great cloaks of sable, like proud sombre Spaniards,
And stalk'd from my sight down the dark corridors,
And in the deep stillness — so still, so profoundly —
I surely have heard their strong footfalls retreating.

When the red-curtain'd West has bent red as with
weeping
Low over the couch where the prone day lay dying,
I have stood with brow lifted, confronting the mountains
That held their white faces of snow in the heavens,
And said, "It is theirs to array them so purely,
Because of their nearness to the temple eternal;"
And child-like have said, "They are fair resting-places
For the dear weary dead on their way up to heaven."

But my soul is not with you to-night, mighty mountains:
It is held to the levels of earth by an angel
Far more than a star, earth-fallen or unfallen,
Yet fierce in her follies and head-strong and stronger
Than streams of the sea running in with the billows.

Very well. Let him woo, let him thrust his white
   whiskers
And lips pale and purple with death in between us;
Let her wed, as she wills, for the gold of the gray-
   beard,
And to give in my hand his league-lands and doub-
   loons:
I will set my face for you, O mountains, my brothers,
For I yet have my honor, my conscience and freedom,
My fleet-footed mustang and pistols rich-silver'd;
I will turn as the earth turns her back on the sun,
But return to the light of her eyes never more,
While red noons have a night and white seas have a
   shore.

   INA, *approaching, offers him her hand.*

     INA.

I have come, dear Don Carlos, to say you farewell.
I shall wed with Don Castro at dawn of to-morrow,
And be all his own — firm, honest, and faithful.
I have promised this thing; that I will keep my
   promise
You who do know me care never to question.
I have master'd myself to say this thing to you

As a hunter would master an hungerèd grizzly.
Hear me : be strong, then, and say me farewell.
The world is his own who will brave its bleak hours.
Dare, then, to confront the cold days in their column;
As they march down upon you, stand, hew them to
    pieces,
One after one, as you would a fierce foeman,
Till not one abideth between two true bosoms.

  Here, standing here, in the vines by the twilight,
While the fair moon was resting her face pure and
    pallid
On the broad breast of heaven as one that is weary,
And her yellow hair trail'd bridal veils down upon us,
And the merry stars play'd hide-and-seek in the
    heaven,
And danced there and dangled like to golden threads
    tangled,
He said to me this : "I am old and am heirless,
And should I die so, by Mejico's statutes
My gold and my broad reach of lands do go forfeit
To the State, in despite of my will or my wishes;
But you, my true wife, would be left my fair widow,
A queen in your wealth to enrich a young lover."

Then I told to him all — all my love and my struggles;
And he called me most brave, and most true, and most
  noble,
And said that he knew all my yearnings already,
And only sought thus with his wealth to endow me.
So then I promised, and shall keep my promise
True as the sun keeps his course in the heaven,
As stainless and pure, yet as warm as the summer.

Let us part as true friends, with a hope all unutter'd;
Without strife or a word, or an ill will between us.
Turn you to the right or the left like to Abram:
The world is before us, come cloud, or come sky;
Give your hand here in mine and say bravely, Good-by.
  [DON CARLOS *with a laugh of scorn flies from the verandah,
  mounts his steed, and disappears.*

INA (*looking out into the night, after a long silence*).

How doleful the night-hawk screams high in the
  heavens,
How dismally gibbers the gray coyoté!
Afar to the south now the red-tongued thunder,
Mine equal brother, my soul's own companion,
Talks low in his sleep, like a giant deep-troubled;

Talks fierce in accord with my own stormy spirit.
But beyond him the supple California lion
Has aroused him up in a dangerous rivalry —
The beast, I could beard him alone in his lair,
And toy with his mane, though it toss'd like a fire.

Scene II.

A spur of Mount Hood overlooking the Willamette river. LAMONTE, *a mountaineer, pitches his solitary camp for the night, and contemplates the scene.*

Lamonte.

A FLUSHED and weary messenger a-west
   Is standing at the half-closed door of day,
As he would say, Good-night; and now his bright
Red cap he tips to me and turns his face.
Were it an unholy thing to say, An angel
Beside the door stood with uplifted seal?
Behold the door seal'd with that blood-red seal
Now burning, spreading o'er the mighty West.
Never again shall the dead day arise
Therefrom, but must be born and come anew.

The tawny, solemn Night, child of the East,
Her mournful robes trails on the distant woods,

And comes this way with firm and stately step.
Afront, and very high, she wears her shining
Breastplate of silver, and on her dark brow
The radiant Venus burns like flashing wit.
Behold! how in her gorgeous flow of hair
Glitter a million mellow yellow gems,
Spilling their molten gold on the dewy grass.
Throned on the boundless plain, and gazing down
Calmly upon the red-seal'd tomb of day,
Resting her form against the Rocky Mountains,
She rules with silent power a peaceful world.

'Tis midnight now. The bent and broken moon,
Batter'd and black, as from a thousand battles,
Hangs silent on the purple walls of heaven.
The angel warrior, guard of the gates eternal,
In battle-harness girt, sleeps on the field;
But when to-morrow comes, when wicked men
That fret the patient earth are all astir,
He will resume his shield, and, facing earthward,
The gates of heaven guard from sins of earth.

'Tis morn. Behold the kingly Day now leaps
The eastern wall of earth with sword in hand.

Clad in a flowing robe of mellow light,
Like to a king that has regain'd his throne,
He warms his drooping subjects into joy,
That rise rejoiced to do him fealty,
And rules with pomp the universal world.

Far, far down in yon narrow spruce-lined cañon
Is the storm-hid abysm of ghostly darkness.
I see him now, as down and down I peer,
Crouch down, and shrink, and creep still up the gorge,
Like some great beast that would conceal its form
In nervous terror from the gaze of man.
The Willamette flashes back afar,
And down his path of palms goes ever on,
An endless caravan to some fair Mecca.
On either side he spreads his yellow vales
With strips of foamy streams and fringe of green,
As a merchant of the storied East unfolds
His gorgeous wealth of green and yellow silks.

'Tis harvest time, and valiant Nature bears
Upon earth's broad and never-failing bosom
A yellow shield of bright and gleaming gold,

Wrought out by patient husbandman to guard
His sturdy race against the hosts of famine.

Lifting the purple curtains of the gods
With flashing helmets that defy the clouds,
And make fierce fellowship with undimm'd stars, —
Mount Hood! and fair Saint Helens! snows eternal
As the sun, — from this my mossy mountain throne,
With lifted and uncover'd head, I greet ye!

Soft snowy breasts on Nature's swelling bosom —
Nature benign and bounteous — let me draw
Pure inspiration from ye, as a child
Draws nurture from a loving mother's breast,
And be your child, your yearning, wayward child,
And, sitting here as on a parent's knee,
Gaze wonder-full into the face of Nature.

Don Carlos *ascends the mountain gesticulating and talking to himself.*

Don Carlos.

Oh for a name that black-eyed maids would sigh
And lean with parted lips at mention of,
That I should seem so tall in the minds of men

That I might walk beneath the arch of Heaven,
And pluck the ripe red stars as I pass'd on,
As favour'd guests do pluck the purple grapes
That hang above the humble entrance-way
Of a palm-thatch'd mountain-inn of Mexico.
Oh, I would give the green leaves of my life
For something grand and real — undream'd deeds!
To wear a mantle, broad and richly jewell'd
As purple heaven fringed with gold at sunset;
To wear a crown as dazzling as the sun,
And, holding up a sceptre lightning-charged,
Stride out among the stars as I have strode
A barefoot boy among the buttercups.
Alas! I am so restless. There is that
Within me doth rebel and rise against
The all I am and half I see in others;
And were 't not for contempt of coward act
Of flying all defeated from the world,
As if I feared and dared not face its ills,
I should ere this have known, known more or less
Than any flesh that frets this sullen earth.
I know not where such thoughts will lead me to:
I have had a fear that they would drive me mad,
And then have flatter'd my weak self, and said

The soul's outgrown the body — yea, the soul
Aspires to the stars, and in its struggles
Does make the dull flesh quiver like an aspen.

LAMONTE.

What waif is this cast here upon my shore,
From seas of subtle and uncertain men?

DON CARLOS.

Subtle and selfish men! — ah, that's the term!
And if you be but earnest in your spleen,
And the other sex across man's shoulders curse,
I'll stand beside you on this crag and curse
And hurl my clench'd fists down upon their heads,
Till I am hoarse as yonder cataract.

LAMONTE.

Why, no, my friend, I'll not consent to that.
No true man yet has ever cursed a woman;
And I — I do not hate my fellow man.
For man by nature bears within himself
Nobility that makes him half a god;
But as in somewise he hath made himself,

His universal thirst for gold and pomp,
And purchased fleeting fame and bubble honors,
Forgetting good, neglecting helpless age,
And rushing rough-shod over lowly merit,
I hold him but a sorry worm indeed;
And so have turn'd me quietly aside
To know the majesty of peaceful woods.
There is a freshness there, a perfect fairness,
A candor and unlanguaged harmony
That wins you, and you worship unawares.

Don Carlos (*as if alone*).

The fabled fount of youth led many fools,
Zealous in its pursuit, to hapless death;
And yet this thirst for fame, this hot ambition,
This soft-toned syren-tongue, enchanting Fame,
Doth lead me headlong on to equal folly,
Like to a wild bird charm'd by shining coils
And swift mesmeric glare of deadly snake:
I would not break the charm, but win a world
Or die with curses blistering my lips.

Lamonte.

You startle me! I am unused to hear

Men talk these fierce and bitter thoughts; and yet
In closed recesses of my soul was once
A dark and gloomy chamber where they dwelt.
Give up ambition — yea, crush out such thoughts
As you would crush from hearth a scorpion-brood:
For, mark me well, they'll get the mastery,
And drive you on to death — or worse, across
A thousand ruin'd homes and broken hearts.

Don Carlos.

Give up ambition! Oh, rather than die,
And glide a lonely, nameless, shivering ghost
Down the dark tide of utter nothingness,
I'd write a name in blood and orphans' tears.
The temple-burner wiser was than kings.
Yet violence is not my inner nature:
I would embalm my name in noblest good,
Would die a death of lofty self-denial,
If but the world beheld the sacrifice
And men took note and told my fame to her,
That she might weep for spite and envy me
My sweet applause and dignity of death.
I'd write a song eternal as the sun,

As chaste and beautiful as is the moon,
That men might read even as they read the stars
In their enamell'd setting in the ring
Above, the crescent blue, in deep delight;
Denied the art and opportunity,
I'd leap strong arm'd upon the centre stage
Of this uncertain, accidental life,
Snatch up the slacken'd reins, and ruthless guide
The idle energies of the monster mob,
Reckless of every cost or pain to man,
To my grand honor, glory and renown,
While he should wonder, worship, call me wise.

LAMONTE.

But would you dare the curse of man and —

DON CARLOS.
       Dare!
I'd dare the curses of the sceptred kings!
I'd build a pyramid of the whitest skulls,
And step therefrom unto the spotted moon,
And thence to stars, thence to the central suns;
Then with one grand and mighty leap would land

Unhinder'd on the shores of the gods of old,
And, sword in hand, unbared and unabash'd,
Would stand forth in the presence of the God
Of gods; there, on the jewell'd inner-side
The walls of heaven, carve with a Damascus
Steel, highest up, a grand and titled name
That time nor tide could touch or tarnish ever.
Yea, any thing on earth, in hell or heaven,
Rather than lie a nameless clod forgot,
Letting stern Time in triumph forward tramp
Above my tombless and neglected dust.

LAMONTE.

Seek not to crop above the heads of men
To be a better mark for envy's shafts.
Come to my peaceful home, and leave behind
These stormy thoughts and daring aspirations.
It is revenge that shows the savage heart,
And earthly power's a thing comparative.
Is not a petty chief of some lone isle,
With half-a-dozen nude and starving subjects,
As much a king as he the Czar of Rusk?
In yonder sweet retreat and balmy place

I 'll abdicate, and you be chief indeed.
There you will reign and tell me of the world,
Its life and lights, its sins and sickly shadows.
The pheasant will reveillé beat at morn,
And rouse us to the battle of the day.
My swarthy subjects will in circle sit,
And, gazing on your kingly presence, deem
You great indeed, and call you chief of chiefs;
And, knowing no one greater than yourself
In all the leafy borders of your realm,
'Gainst what can pride or poor ambition chafe?

'Twill be a kingdom without king, save you,
Broader than that the cruel Cortes won,
With subjects truer than he ever knew,
That know no law but only Nature's law,
And no religion know but that of love.
There truth and beauty are, for there is Nature,
Serene and simple. She will be our priestess,
And in her calm and uncomplaining face
We will read well her rubric and be wise.

A glass-like lake lies on this mountain-top;
You bend you o'er, and, resting on your palms,

Gaze down and down full fifty fathoms deep,
And see the speckled mountain-trout that sport,
All gold and silver-sheathed and scaled, above
Rich palaces, brown, marble-built and massive,
Hewn out and built or ever man had named
The stars — when mighty Nimrod kept the chase.

Black, quilless pines, perfect as those ashore —
Proportion'd mighty, perfectly erect —
Stand dark and sullen in the silent courts.
You cast a pebble in, a nut in size,
And watch it wind and wind a weary time,
Then see it plain as if 'twas in your hand.
Could you believe a flood could be so pure,
So mirror-like, so strangely beautiful?
Some tall pines press up to the water's edge
And droop adown their plumed and sable heads,
And weep above their buried comrades still
All night the dewy tears of Nature.

A league across, the pines have broken rank
And stand in small platoons, or stand alone;
While far across the rolling sea-like meads
Do dash and wheel the spotted Indian steeds.

The warriors shout and gallop up and down,
And lovely maids in beaded moccasons,
Furs thick with red and yellow feathers fringed,
As tall and straight as water tulés are,
Go forth in dusky beauty in their walk
Beneath the circling shadows of the pines,
Or bathe and dream along the borders of the lake.

And far beyond, where pines crowd thick and tall,
And waters dwindle to a narrow wedge,
The glad lake opes her pretty gushing mouth,
And down a foaming cataract of silver
Pours all her ceaseless song and melody —
The far source of the lovely Willamette.

At night, o'erspread by the rich, purple robe,
The deep imperial Tyrian hue that folds
The invisible form of the Eternal God,
You will see the sentry stars come marching forth
And take their posts upon the field above,
Around the great white tent where sleeps their chief;
You will hear the kakea singing in a dream
The wildest, sweetest song a soul can drink.
And when the tent is folded up, and all

The golden-fringed red sentries faced about
To let the pompous day-king pass along,
We two will stand upon a sloping hill,
Where white-lipped springs come leaping, laughing up,
With water spouting forth in merry song
Like bridled mirth from out a school-girl's throat.
And look far down the bending Willamette,
And in his thousand graceful curves and strokes
And strânge meanderings, men misunderstand,
Read the unutterable name of GOD.

DON CARLOS.

Why, truly now, this fierce and broken land,
Seen through your eyes, assumes a fairer shape.
Lead up, for you are nearer God than I.

SCENE III.

INA, *in black, alone by the sea. Midnight.*

INA.

WEEP? Me to weep? How I laugh to think
of it!
I lift my dark brow to the breath of the ocean,
Soft kissing me now like the lips of my mother,

And laugh low and long as I crush the brown grasses,
To think I should weep! Why, I never wept — never,
Not even in punishments dealt me in childhood!
Yea, all of my wrongs and my bitterness buried
In my brave baby heart, all alone and unfriended.
And I pitied, with proud and disdainfulest pity,
The weak who would weep, and I laugh'd at the folly
Of those who could laugh and make merry with play-
    things:
Then I tuck'd down my chin and went under the
    lindens,
And made me companions of grave hornéd cattle.

No! I will not weep now over that I desired.
Desired? Yes: I to myself dare confess it,
Ah, too, to the world should it question too closely,
And bathe me and sport in a deep sea of candor.
Bah! Cowards deceive, and I know not what fear is.
Men lie, who lack courage to tell truth — the cowards!

Like Lucifer dower'd with pride and wild beauty,
With poverty cursed and the fiercest ambition,
I stood all alone by my sweet child-mother;

When the kind dotard came and did bend him forward,
Fast thrusting his beard by my boy Don Carlos.
And so I did wed him. Would you know now the reason?
I endured the cold frost for the springtime to follow,
Did wed to the one for the love of the other,
And to get for him gold, gave my whole fair body.

Oh, alone and unlike to all other things earthly
Was my brave boy-lover; as an isle 'mid the oceans
Of men, so alike as are drops of water.
He did win my heart by his great defiance
Of men and manners, and his thoughts unbridled.
But now made a queen, after all my struggles,
I shall seek him out and surprise and enrich him;
And seek him with songs as a sweet boy-poet.
I did bear my burden long, loyal and faithful,
Even down to the end, and did make no murmur:
But now he is dead and I dare joy at it.
And am I then the first that has joy'd thus fiercely,
And held Death's mantle while he did his office?

What now if the odds were but this wild courage,
That does dare shape thought into plainest language!

Let the world be deceived: it insists upon it;
Let it bundle me round in its black woe-garments;
But I, self with self — my free soul fearless —
Am as frank as the sun, nor the toss of a copper
Care I if the world call it good or evil.
I am glad to-night, and in new-born freedom
Forget all earth with my old companions, —
The moon and the stars and the moon-clad ocean.
I am face to face with the stars that know me,
And gaze as I gazed in the eyes of my mother,
Forgetting the city and the coarse things in it;
For there's naught but God in the shape of mortal,
Save one — my wandering, wild boy-lover —
That I do esteem worth a stale banana.

The air hangs heavy and is warm on my shoulder,
And is thick with odors of balm and blossom;
The great bay sleeps with the ships on her bosom.
Through the Golden Gate, to the left-hand yonder,

INA. 153

The white sea lies in a deep sleep, snoring,
The father of melody, the mother of measure,
Lifting his breast to the moon, deep breathing. —
Let me sing by the sea a song as he slumbers,
A song to the air of the sweetest of singers.
[*Sings.*

O tempest-toss'd sea of white bosoms,
O breasts with demands and desires,
O hearts fill'd of fevers, of fires,
Reaching forth from the tangible blossoms,
Reaching far for impossible things!
Beat not, O break not your warm wings
On the cruel cold bars any more.
Lo! the sea, the great sea has his shore,
And lies in his limit; the moon
Has her night, and the sun has his noon.

What a wonderful world truly this is!
How barren of wisdom and worth!
How populous full is the earth
Of the fools that taste not of its blisses!
Then despise not the glories before you,

With your feet on the things that are real:
Take the tangible loves that adore you,
Touch the forms that are flesh and can feel.

Leaves fade, and the frosts are before us;
Leaves fall, and the winter winds are;
Loves fail! Let us cross and deplore us;
Loves die! Lift your hands as at war.
Lift your hands to the world and deny it;
Lift your voice, cry aloud and deny;
Cry aloud, "'Tis a lie!" and belie it
With lives made a beautiful lie.

Scene IV.

A Wood by a rivulet on a spur of Mount Hood, overlooking the Columbia. Lamonte *and* Don Carlos, *on their way to the camp, have met with other hunters, and are reposing under the shadow of the forest. Some deer are observed descending to the brook, and one of the party seizes his rifle.*

Don Carlos.

NAY, then, my friend, don't strike them from your covert.

Strike like a serpent in the grass conceal'd?
What, steal into their homes, and, when athirst
And unsuspecting, they come down in couples
And dip their muzzles in the mossy brink,
Then shoot them down without a chance to fly —
The only means that God has given them,
Poor, unarm'd mutes, to baffle cruel man!
Ah, now I see you had not thought of this!
The hare is fleet, and quick at sight and sound,
His coat is changed with color of the fields;
Yon deer turn brown when forest-leaves are brown;
The dog has teeth, the cat has teeth and claws,
And man has craft and art and sinewy arms:
All things that live have some means of defence . . .

Lucus.

Ay, all — save only lovely, helpless woman.

Don Carlos.

Nay, woman has her tongue — arm'd to the teeth.

Lucus.

Thou Timon, what can 'scape your bitterness?
But for this sweet repose and peace of Nature,

Upon whose breast we here recline and dream,
Why, you might lift your voice and rail at her!

Don Carlos.

Oh, I am out of patience with your faith!
What! Nature quiet, peaceful, uncomplaining?
I've seen her fretted like a lion caged,
Chafe like a peevish woman cross'd and churl'd,
Tramping and foaming like a whelpless bear;
Have seen her weep till earth was wet with tears,
Then turn all smiles — a jade that won her point;
Have seen her tear the hoary hair of Ocean,
While he, himself full half a world, would moan
And roll and toss his clumsy hands all day
To earth like some great helpless babe, that lay
Rude-rock'd and cradled by an unseen nurse,
Then stain her snowy hem with salt-sea tears;
And when the peaceful, mellow moon came forth,
To walk and meditate among the yellow
Blooms that make blest the upper purple fields,
This wroth dyspeptic sea ran after her
With all his soul, as if to pour himself,
All sick and helpless, in her snowy lap.

Content! Oh, she has crack'd the ribs of earth
And made her shake poor trembling man from off
Her back, even as a grizzly shakes the hounds;
She has upheaved her rocky spine against
The flowing robes of the Eternal God.
Nature is not content. Ha! I have heard her
Rushing at night swift down the streaming plain,
And, when the storm was thick and deep at night,
Have seen her press her face in blacken'd mask
Against my window-pane, and sob, and weep,
And wail, until the great round tears ran down;
And then, as if in savage desperation,
Seize violent hold and shake the sash and frame
Until they quailed and quaked like aspen-leaf.
I did unbar the window for her once,
This wild-lamenting, fretful, childish Nature:
She, like a wood-rear'd girl, rush'd reckless in
And hid her trembling in a darken'd corner.
Peer down there, half a league by cliff and bough,
Into the river's white complaining face,
And see his gray hair trail'd in shifting sands:
There comes a wail of terror aud despair
Up from his white and trembling lips a-foam,
While he uplifts his thin white palms to pines

That bend dark-brow'd and sad as o'er a tomb.
No! 'tis a pretty thought and pretty theme
That Nature reigns in majesty serene:
But lift the skirts of Isis, and be wise.

Lucus.

Heartless ambition and unholy pride!
Hatred of man and strange contempt of woman!
At war with all, and your own enemy!
While man is man, do not attempt to shine
Too bright: consult your peace, beware of pride;
For malice shoots alone at shining marks.
Beware of pride. I once did hear a learn'd
Man say, "By pride the angels fell from heaven."

Don Carlos.

By pride they reach'd a place from which to fall.

Lucus.

And were they better, happier, having thus
Ascended, then prostrate to fall so far?

Don Carlos.

Yes! Let me only win the love I woo,

Enjoy her but one brief hour, then lose all,
I will be winner that one gracious hour;
And in my memory then will I possess
A wall'd spring hung about with cooling palms,
Where weary recollection traversing
The barren desert of my life, might pause
And bathe herself, and, resting, rise refresh'd.
There be some men with hope so full and strong,
Their souls feed on the future — a green field —
But mine will not go on, but backward turns
As if for something lost or left behind :
Goes back against my will, an endless lane,
A stray sheep from the flock that ever keeps
The dusty centre of the unwater'd way,
And looks up weary at the fasten'd gates
That lead to cooling springs and verdant banks,
But closed against me when at first I pass'd.

LUCUS.

There was one once of nature like to this :
He stood a barehead boy upon a cliff
Pine-crown'd, that hung high o'er a bleak north sea;
His long hair stream'd and flash'd like yellow silk,
His sea-blue eyes lay deep and still as lakes

O'erhung by mountains arched in virgin snow;
And far astray, and friendless and alone,
A tropic bird blown through the north frost-wind,
He stood above the sea in the cold white moon,
His thin face lifted to the flashing stars,
And talk'd familiarly full face to face
With the Eternal God, in solemn night,
Confronting Him with free and flippant air
As one confronts a merchant o'er his counter,
And in his vehement blasphemy did say:
"God, put aside this world — show me another!
God, this world is a cheat — hand down another!
I will not buy — not have it as a gift.
Put it aside and hand me down another —
Another, and another, still another,
Till I have tried the fairest world that hangs
Upon the walls and broad dome of your shop,
The finest one that has come from your hand;
For I am proud of soul and regal born,
And will not have a cheap and cheating world."

Don Carlos.

The noble youth! So God gave him another?

Lucus.

What, he, the poor blasphemous and crazy beggar!
So must you speak, or else the world will hiss you,
Of these brave spirits God tries in His fire,
Then takes unto Himself, as guards in heaven —
Loves them and takes them as his own companions
In their strong youth, as the old Greeks have said,
Leaving their dust in tracts most desolate.
A bear, as in old time, came from the woods
And tore him there upon that storm-swept cliff —
A grim and grizzled bear, like unto hunger.
A tall ship sail'd adown the sea next morn,
And, standing with his glass upon the prow,
The captain saw a vulture on a cliff,
Gorging, and pecking, stretching his long neck,
Bracing his raven plumes against the wind,
Fretting the tempest with his sable feathers.

Don Carlos.

'Twas wrong, he should have lived and fought it out.
This nursing a gushing heart of sentiment
Does bring contempt on half the schemes of life.
Tears are a woman's weapons, sorry things

Even in her, but in man despicable.
What! lie down and be rode upon rough-shod?
No! face and fight, and be at least respected.
The lion is not a comely beast, but brave,
And is therefore revered above all beasts,
And, bravest of the brave, is chosen king.
God and his angels fought for heaven; Christ
Did beat with thongs the craven money-changers;
The chosen Peter wore a willing sword.
The stormy elements war through all the year;
Spring and bluff Winter strive for mastery;
Autumn and Winter struggle on the heath,
And I have seen them wrestle in the woods
Until the yellow leaves were all awhirl,
And sighs and groans went up and down the hills.

He sought the impossible — asked good unmix'd,
Asked peace on earth where there is no peace.
Here do the kernel and the chaff all blend,
And good and evil intwine. Hereafter,
After the harvest, the segregation.
Even the Christ, two thousand years ago,
In the far dawn while yet the world was young,

Newer, and purer from the hand of God,
Did find a traitor in His chosen twelve.

LAMONTE.

There's that in you that draws my soul to yours;
Your head, I fear, but not your heart, is wrong.
I will not answer now, but summon you
To yon grand courts to give in evidence,
Where sleep the monarchs of a thousand storms,
For ever still in shrouds of color'd moss,
While green vines twine a pretty wreath above,
As crowning graves of dear and gallant dead;
The Yew, in cloak of everlasting green,
Does sweep her pretty palms in winning eloquence,
While scarlet berries bead her lisping boughs
Like threaded drops of rainbow-painted dew,
Or pearls upon an Indian maiden's limbs.
Reposing there on couch of mossy carpet,
Where darkest green is wove with yellow moss,
And yellow wove with green, all undisturb'd
By sight or sound save birds of sweetest song,
While mighty trees above receive the red
And hot darts of the sun on bearded helmets,

Will come to you the higher evidence,
Stronger a thousandfold and more convincing
Than if produced by oath of all mankind.
With me in my untraversed wilds and caves,
My kingdom unexplored, you will read the book
Of Nature that unclasp'd lies, while the winds
Mesmeric as the fingers of your love
Will turn the living leaves as you read on —
Will paint in lambent amber hues and Tyrian,
And strike in plaintive mellow tone a harp
That hangs upon the lightning-shiver'd pine;
And, reading, we shall happier grow and better.
Nature will mightier seem yet milder there,
Because we shall be nearer to her face.

Don Carlos.

And if I should, what then? What though I met
My Maker face to face, as in the Mount?
Left mountain-bound in islands of the clouds,
What fame or fortune could betide me there?
I had as well know secrets of deep death,
Or hold in hand the keys of Cæsar's coffers,
And be for evermore forbid their use.

Lamonte.

Why, no! You'd gather up pure gems of thought,
Or catch bright fancies one by one that flit
You by like beauteous Orient birds, and cage
Them up between a precious volume's lids;
Or like one gathering gold from out the sand,
A little here, a little there, then all
Mould in one bright and shining shield, and so
Bearing it up, descend upon the world
Like some proud conqueror of olden time;
Or shine forth in the newness of your thought
Like some bright lovely star that hastens forth
Before its mates, chasing the sullen sun,
And so be seen and known of all the world.

Don Carlos.

What is there new atop of this old world?
Should e'er I come to write your books, why I
Would search among the quaint and dusty tomes
While the selfish world sought pleasure and repose,
And Shoddy did up the European tour
Much as a blockhead schoolboy does a task,
While men well skill'd in sales of soap and lard,

And learn'd in all the art of packing pork,
Would coarsely tramp the sacred dust that deeds,
When earth was blithe and young, have made immortal
(Where I would softly tread unshod and bared).
I 'd pick up here and there from dusty masters
The ancient coins of loftiest, noblest thought,
And cast them in one shining shield of bronze,
And bearing it aloft high-heralded,
Well flank'd with sheets of broad advertisements,
Be call'd a bard of new-inspired song.
I 'd throttle modest mien and word in this
Swift age, as base traducers of my fame;
I 'd cast meek modesty into the sea,
The Jonah that had brought me all my trouble.
I 'd plant a preface full afront my book
As you would plant a battery in war,
And, bearing down all things that dared oppose,
With shout and flourish take the world by storm.
Or at the least I 'd hold a touching tale
Before my book as you would hold a shield,
And with it catch or turn aside the darts
And poison'd shafts of killing criticism.
But mind you, fame is not now won with ink,

The author's pen's a lever, lifting others;
The stain of blood is readier seen from far,
And gold like some bright star's at once beheld
By all the world throughout the darkest day,
And instant wins the worship of the mob.

The world has turn'd shopkeeper — go, sell, sell;
Put on yourself a costly price, to sell:
Real cash-customers buy no cheap goods.
The mob has now got hold the money-bags,
And skilful judges of corn, pork, and cabbage
Do judge men by their arrogance and name.
Assume a lofty air and sounding title —
The barefaced fools outnumber and outshout
The men of sense and solid worth and thought.
The gilded chisell'd vessels that encase
Most stupid, sour, and unwholesome wines
At once are pluck'd at by the money-mob,
The while the plain but precious bottled liquor
Accumulates the dust of generations.

Go, buy and sell. Get gold. A golden lever
Moves more than e'er the Syracusan might.
Deceit brings wealth, wealth buys the bubble fame,

Fame lulls the fever of the soul, and makes
Us feel that we have grasp'd an immortality.

Oh, I have mock'd at man and shook with mirth.
Yet is in all a sort of savage justice.
Have you no time observed with what an odd
Yet an impartial hand are things divided?
The fool has fortunes thrust upon him, while
The man of brains is pinch'd with penury.
The dolt who feels as much of sentiment
As a milch-cow, fed in her field of clover,
Goes on serene through sweetest-smelling meads,
With maidens fainting for a breath of love,
And heiresses cast at his empty head
By fond mammas, whene'er he please to show it;
While he of finest sense is blown by fate,
Like some sea-waif, upon the frontier wild.
The prettiest maiden is a screeching parrot,
While she of wit is shorn of all of beauty;
The gifted man is stoop'd and sallow-pale,
The ass stands six feet up of lovely flesh;
Wisdom means age and gout and ugliness,
While the crude boy has health and ruddy beauty,
And wisdom's sov'reign head is bow'd and bald,
And the rich man envies the beggar's stomach.

LAMONTE.

Give me your hand, your right in this my left —
Its blood comes nearer from the heart; and then,
My right is dead, deader than this your love;
For love, like Lazarus, can only sleep,
But, breathed upon by love and hope, will rise —
Rise up a loftier and a holier love.
I know you now; I am an elder brother,
For sorrow and deceit have made us kin.
From want and disappointment, bitter breasts,
We two have drawn our stormy natures.

A Young HUNTER *ascends the mountain and approaches.*

DON CARLOS.

Ho! whom, now, have we here? Talk of the devil,
And he is at hand. Say, who are you, and whence?

HUNTER.

I am a poet, and dwell down by the sea.

DON CARLOS.

A poet! a poet, forsooth! Fool! hungry fool!
Would you know what it means to be a poet?

It is to want a friend, to want a home,
A country, money, — ay, to want a meal.
It is not wise to be a poet now,
For the world has so fine and modest grown
It will not praise a poet to his face,
But waits till he is dead some hundred years,
Then uprears marbles cold and stupid as itself.

But rest you here, and while the red-hot sun
Wheels on, and sleep my friends beneath the boughs,
Do, pray, beguile the hour with a song.

Hunter (*sings*).

I am as one unlearned, uncouth,
From country come to join the youth
Of some sweet town in quest of truth;
  A Nazarene of wood and plain
A-west, from whence no good may come.
I stand apart as one that's dumb.
I hope — I fear — I hasten home.
  I plunge into my wilds again.

I catch some dulcet symphonies,
I drink the low sweet melodies

That stream through dense dark feathered trees
   Like echoes from some far church bell,
Or music on the water spilled
Beneath the still moon's holy spell,
And life is sweeter — all is well —
   The soul is fed. The heart is filled.

I move among my frowning firs,
Black bats wheel by in rippled whirs,
While naught else living breathes or stirs.
   I peep — I lift the boughs apart —
I tiptoe up — I try to rise —
I strive to gaze into the eyes
Of charmers charming very wise —
   I coin their faces on my heart.

I hear them on the Northern hills
Discoursing with the beaded rills,
While over all the full moon spills
   Her flood in gorgeous plenilune.
White skilful hands sweep o'er the strings,
I heed as when a seraph sings,
I lean to catch the whisperings,
   I list into the night's sweet noon.

I see them by the Eastern strand,
A singing sea-shell in each hand,
And silk locks tossing as they stand,
  And tangled in the toying breeze.
And lo! the sea with salty tears,
While white hands toss, then disappear,
Doth plead that they for years and years
  Will stay and sing unto the seas.

Don Carlos.

Hold! hold your tongue, and hold my aching head!
'Tis well for you the Roman mob is dead.
This stuff of yours is full of pompous I's
As a candidate for Congress is of lies.
Why talk so loudly of yourself at large?
Your neighbors do that for you, free of charge!
This poetry's not of the heart, but stomach;
Not inspiration, but 'tis indigestion
Disturbs the balance-wheel that rules your brain.
Love food the less — respect your stomach more,
For more have groan'd and died from over-use
Of knives and forks, than ever fell in war
By bloody sword and bayonet and ball.
        [*The* Hunter *rises and moves away.*

Don Carlos.

Why, what's the haste? You'll reach there soon
    enough.

Hunter.

Reach where?

Don Carlos.

The Inn to which all earthly roads do tend:
The "neat apartments furnish'd — see within;"
The "furnish'd rooms for quiet, single gentlemen;"
The narrow six-by-two where you will lie
With cold blue nose pointing up to the grass,
Labell'd and box'd, and ready all for shipment.
'Twas said of old that all roads led to Rome,
But all roads now do lead to this small Inn.
'Tis just so many leagues ahead of you,
Why, then, make haste to cross the space between?

Scene V.

Lamonte's *Camp-fire in the Mountains.*

Don Carlos, Lamonte, *the* Hunter, *and others, seated around, smoking and telling tales of home and how they came to take to the Mountains.*
Old Lamonte, *the mountaineer, lounging at one side, talking with the Young Hunter, and pointing out to him his new companions:* —

I GREET you welcome to these wild mountains,
   As will these my comrades at their good leisure.
And now, meantime, that you'll know them better,
Yon fair-hair'd man, all in beaded buckskin
And belt of wampum, now peering skyward,
Is noble young Lucus, a heart-sick lover
That has fled a coward from the shafts of Cupid,
Fearing far less the red Indians' arrows.
The man beyond him, thick-lipp'd and surly,
'Tis said, is a patriot from merry old England
Who took to these mountains for the good of his
   country.
To the left, by the pine, is a dollarless marquis
At talk with a scholar high-bred, of Oxford,
Self-exiled, say, for some gay peccadillo.

Beyond, in the shade, is a Southern gentleman
Talking with one of his ten brown women.
That black Kanuk, with his hair on his shoulders,
Has herds and leagues on the North Red River,
And wigwams alive with olive-hued children.
Over here, with his pipe, is a thoughtfullest German,
Profound, it is said, in his lore and letters,
And silent in all of the tongues of Europe.
Yon fast young man, with a rose in his bosom,
Is a Spaniard waiting for a dear relation
To die, to come to his hard-earn'd fortune.
And last I name is a long-nosed Yankee,
Shrewdly watching to improve his chances,
Ready to trade, trap, preach, or peddle.
Such are the men of the rough Rocky Mountains,
Not hairy monsters as some do pronounce us,
But men blown up from the world's four quarters,
Gentle or vicious, serene or savage,
Common alone in undoubted courage.
Hist! list and learn, as they tell their adventures.

A gray FRENCHMAN *ends a tale thus:* —

Alas, the sight I saw that night!
Alas, that I should tremble here!

I know 'tis not a coward fear,
And yet I shiver as in fright.

The blue fields blossom'd yellow bloom
Of brilliants set in purple gloom,
A silver shield slid on and on
Between me and the better land,
And I was glad. I kiss'd my hand
To melting stars and mellow moon —
I left the full feast oversoon,
And sought the peerless paragon.
Gay jesting at her clever art
In hiding in some spot unknown,
I sought her, thought her mine, my own —
I had despised a baser thought.
I sought her as I would be sought
With boundless faith and beating heart,
Fill'd full of sweet uncertainties,
Among the moonlit, fruited trees.

Alas, the sight I saw that night
Through stripèd bars of streaming light,
And boughs that whisper'd plaintively
In solemn sympathy with me!

A red dead leaf was in her hair,
Full half a swelling breast was bare,
And mad disorder everywhere.
And, gliding through a thorny brake
And sliding like a slimy snake,
I saw him stooping steal away
Like serpent caught in Paradise,
That hid it from the face of day
With guilty and unholy eyes.

I saw a sight that night, that night,
Because I could not help but see —
Because the moon was bleached so white —
Because the stars were yellow light —
Because they blossom'd in a tree
And dropp'd their blossoms on the grass —
And saw because, alas, alas!
An evil spirit guided me.

He was my friend. He ate my bread.
He counsell'd very wise and well;
"I love you more than words can tell,"
He many and many a time had said.
He suck'd the juices from my fruit

And left for me the bitter rind.
I am not crazed — it was unkind
To suck the sweetness from my fruit
And give me back the bitter rind.

And did I curse or crush or kill?
Go down to yonder wooded gate,
Go down, go down, it groweth late;
You hesitate and hesitate —
I tremble as if in a chill.

It open'd very wide that night,
For two went through — but one return'd:
And when its rusty hinges turn'd,
They creak'd as if in pain or fright.

Three finger-prints are on the bar —
Three finger-prints of purple gore.
You scan my hand — here, scan it more,
And count my fingers o'er and o'er,
You cannot see a sign of gore.
I lost one finger in the war,
And is it not an honor'd scar?

Don Carlos.

Woman! and still the sad burden is woman!
O most valiant, most gallant gentleman,
Frighten'd from home by the flirt of a petticoat!
Well, sigh to the moon and delight in delusions,
And dream that she too turns a pale face to heaven.
Bah! barely your shadow goes out from her threshold
Before she is turning all smiles on another.
But you, yon gray trapper there, storm-stained and grizzled,
And gazing still dreamily into the fire,
Sure you have a tale without burden of woman.
Come, call your far thoughts from the mountain or plain,
In the wars with the savage, and fight them again.

The Trapper

(*Still gazing into the fire, and speaking in a low tone as if to himself*).

Back, backward to-night is memory traversing,
Over the desert my weary feet travell'd,
Thick with the wreck of my dear heart-idols
And toppled columns of my ambition,
Red with the best of my hot heart's purple.

This then is all of the sweet life she promised;
This then is all of the fair life I painted!
Dead, ashen apples of the Dead-Sea border!
Ah yes, and worse by a thousand numbers,
Since that can be lifted away as we will it,
While desolate life with its dead hope buried
Clings on to the clay, though the soul despise it.

Down under the hill and there under the fir-tree
By the spring, and looking far out in the valley,
She stands as she stood in the glorious Olden,
Swinging her hat in her right hand dimpled,
The other hand toys with a honey-suckle
That has tiptoed up and is trying to kiss her.
Her dark hair is twining her neck and her temples
As tendrils some beautiful Balize marble.

"O eyes of lustre and love and passion!
O radiant face like the sea-shell tinted!
White cloud with the sunbeams tangled in it!"
I cried, as I stood in the dust beneath her,
And gazed on the goddess my boy-heart worshipped
With a love and a passion, a part of madness.

"Dreamer," she said, and a tinge of displeasure
Swept over her face that I should disturb her,
"All of the fair world is spread out before you;
Go down and possess it with love and devotion,
And heart ever tender and touching as woman's,
And life shall be fair as the first kiss of morning."
I turn'd down the pathway, was blinded no longer:
Another was coming, tall, manly, and bearded.

I built me a shrine in the innermost temple —
In the innermost rim of the heart's red centre —
And placed her therein, sole possessor and priestess,
And carved all her words on the walls of my temple.
They say that he woo'd her there under the fir-tree,
That he won her one eve, when the katydids mock'd
    her.
He may have a maiden and call her Merinda;
But mine is the one that stands there for ever
Leisurely swinging her hat by the ribbons.

They say she is wedded. No, not my Merinda,
For mine stands for ever there under the fir-tree
Gazing and swinging her hat by the ribbons.
They tell me her children reach up to my shoulder.

'Tis false. I did see her down under the fir-tree
When the stars were all busy a-weaving thin laces
Made red with their gold and the moon's yellow tresses,
Swinging her hat as in days of the Olden.

 True, that I spoke not nor ventured to touch her —
Touch her! I sooner would pluck the sweet Mary,
The mother of Jesus, from arms of the priesthood,
As they kneel at the altar in holy devotion!
  * * * * * *
 And was it for this that my heart was kept tender,
Fashion'd from thine, O sacristan maiden? —
That coarse men could pierce my warm heart to the
  purple?
That vandals could enter and burn out its freshness?
That rude men could trample it into the ashes? —
Oh was it for this that my heart was kept open?
I look'd in a glass, not the heart of my fellow,
Whose was the white soul I saw there reflected?
But trample the grape that the wine may flow freely!

 Beautiful priestess, be with me for ever!
You still are secure. They know not your temple,
They never can find it, nor pierce it, nor touch it,

Because in their hearts they know no such temple.
I turned my back on them, a Seminole banished,
Much indeed leaving in dark desolation,
But bearing one treasure alone that is dearer
Than all they possess or have fiercely torn from me:
A maiden that stands looking far down the valley
Swinging her hat by its long, purple ribbons.

Don Carlos.

Worse and worse, and the burden still woman!
The crucifixion of rhyme and of reason,
With the sweet Christ-truth bleeding dead between
    them!
Here you, young rover, or hunter, or poet,
If you have wit, here's a chance to show it;
Give us at least some rhymes that jingle,
Nor jar the soul till the senses tingle.

Hunter (*sings*).

Alone on this desolate border,
On this ruggedest rimm'd frontier,
Where the hills huddle up in disorder
Like a fold in mortal fear,
Where the mountains are out at the elbow

In their yellow coats seedy and sere,
Where the river runs sullen and yellow,
This dismallest day of the year.

I go up and down on the granite,
Like an unholy ghost under bans.
O Christ! for the eloquent quiet!
For the final folding of hands!
What am I? Where am I going,
With these turbulent winds that are blowing?
What sowing of wind in the lands,
And what shall I reap from such sowing?
I look at the lizard that glides
Up over the mossy boulders,
With green epaulets on his shoulders,
And regiment-stripes on his sides.

My feet are in dust to the ankles;
My heart, it is dustier still;
Will never the dust be levell'd
Till the heart is laid under the hill?
I look at the sun sliding over,
A cloud is swinging on hinges
And is trying his glory to cover.

But see! his beams in the fringes
Are tangled and fastened in falling,
And a sailor above us is calling
"Untangle the ravels and fringes."

In grim battle-lines up o'er us
Gray, shapely ships are wheeling,
Hulk, sail, and shroud revealing.
A flash, a crash appalling,
A hurling of red-hot spears,
Hark! terrible thunder calling
In fierce infernal chorus!
Now silver sails are falling
Like silver sheens before us.

What Nelson to fame aspires
In the chartless bluer deep
Where white ships toss and tack?
And what armed host appears?
Lo! I have seen their fires
In blue fields where they sleep
At night, in the bivouac;
And they battle, bleed, and weep,
For this rain is warm as tears.

Oh! why was I ever a dreamer?
Better a brute on the plain,
Or one who believes his redeemer
Is greed, and gold, and gain;
Or one who can riot and revel,
Than be pierced by unbearable pain,
With poesy darling, in travail,
That will not be born from the brain.

O bride by the breathing ocean,
With lustrous and brimming eye,
Pour out the Lethean potion
Till a lustrum rolleth by,
Lulling a soul's commotion,
Plashing against the sky —
Calming a living spectre
With its two hands toss'd on high.

Come to me, darling, adorning
Like Aurora the desolate region;
Come with step stately as morning,
Or come like the march of a legion,
Or come without caution or warning,
Or come like the lordly tycoon,

Or in majesty like to the moon,
But come, and come soon, over-soon.

Are the sea-winds mild and mellow
Where my sun-brown'd babies are,
A-weaving the silken and yellow
Seam'd sunbeams over their hair?
Go on and go on in disorder,
O cloud with the silver-red rim,
While tangled up in your bright border,
The glinting silk sunbeams swim.

DON CARLOS (*yawning*).

Oh! why indulge in such gipsy jargon,
Since maids must mock, and men slay to protect them
A song like to this with a savagest silence?
I fear, young man, you mistake your calling;
Why not fall the forests, plant red potatoes?
Or what of the art of raising green pumpkins,
And tall-topp'd corn with its silks of silver?
Or may be some sheep could endure your measures
On the Yamhill hills, if you must aspire,
As you swing a crook, and so sweep your lyre.

HUNTER.

The bird sings in the busy spring,
The sea sings in his booming swells,
And all his pink and pearly shells
Sing of the sea, and ever sing.
You break the shell or bear it far
From ocean as the morning star,
Yet still it sings, fast bound or free,
In mellow measures, of the sea.
And I shall sing and sing and sing,
Sing ill or well, though men do chide,
Until a hand in mine is laid
To lead unto the other side.
Afar a ploughboy's song is heard,
In chorus with the building bird,
My song is his — his my reward.

I heard a redbreast on the wall,
And then I heard the truants' call,
And cast a storm of earth and stone.
He flew, and perch'd him far and lone,
Above a rushing cataract,
Where never living thing had track'd —

INA.

Where mate nor man nor living thing
Could ever heed or hear him sing;
And there he sang his song of spring,
As if a world were listening.
He sang because he could but sing,
Sweet bird, for he was born to sing.

A million hearts have felt as much
As ever prince of poets told,
With souls that scorn'd a colder touch
Than love refined to finest gold,
Yet drove the team and turn'd the mould,
And whistled songs and tragedies
That would have thrill'd to rage or tears;
The beam and moon their lance and shield,
A moat, the furrow deep and broad;
And lived content through all their years
In one long paradise of peace,
Unheard beyond their broken sod.
And shall I then be less than these?

They kept their fields', their flocks' increase,
And walk'd their ideal world in peace,
They would not drag it down to fit

The mass of men with golden god —
They could not drag man up to it,
So lived and died without complain.
All tuneless in their full refrain,
They break in billows through the sod.

A million poets God hath wrought;
But very few have made pretence,
And fewer still found utterance;
For words are shackles unto thought,
And fancies fetter'd down by words
Droop dull and tame as prison'd birds,
Lose all the bright hues of the sky,
As does the claspèd butterfly.

[*As the* YOUNG HUNTER *concludes,* DON CARLOS *apart, and looking down the mountain to the declining moon, continues:* —]

Well, he would make you a good maid-servant;
I could say, " She can come to you well recommended; "
For behold he has sung till they sleep most soundly.
The thin, sullen moon, pale-faced, and crooked
As a half-starved kine, a most vicious heifer,
Is sliding down in all haste from heaven,

To gore in the flank of yon sleeping mountain.
My comrades sleep, and does sleep all Nature;
The world has a rest and a truce till to-morrow;
There is peace, and surcease of sin and of sorrow;
All things take rest but I —

    HUNTER.
       And I only,
Your minstrel and whilom your roving young hunter.
    [*Loosening his hair from his shoulders.*
Ah me! My Don Carlos, look kindly upon me!
With my hand on your arm and my dark brow lifted
Up level to yours, do you not now know me?
'Tis your own, own INA, you loved by the ocean,
In the warm-spiced winds from the far Cathay.
O welcome me now after all my struggles,
And years of waiting and my weary journeys.

    DON CARLOS (*bitterly*).

"And he received her with his arms extended,
And they were wedded, and lived long and happily" —
At least so runneth the oft-told story.
But life is prosy, and my soul uprises
Against you, madam, as you stand before me

With the smell of the deadman still upon you,
And your dark hair wet from his death-damp forehead.
You are not my Ina, for she is a memory,
A marble chisell'd, in my heart's dark chamber
Set up for ever, and nought can change her;
And you are a stranger, and the gulf between us
Is wide as the Plains, and as deep as Pacific.
No! lips blood-stain'd and your limbs polluted
Shall tempt me not from my lordly mountains.

But now, good-by. In your serape folded,
Hard by in the heat of the pine-knot fire,
Sleep you as sound as you will be secure;
And on the morrow — now mark me, madam —
When to-morrow comes, why, you will turn you
To the right or left as did Father Abram.
Good-night, for ever and for aye, good-by;
My bitter is sweet and your truth is a lie.

  INA (*letting go his arm and stepping back*).
 Well then! 'tis over, and 'tis well thus ended;
I am well escaped from my life's devotion.
The waters of bliss are a waste of bitterness;
The day of joy I did join hands over,

As a bow of promise when my years were weary,
And set high up as a brazen serpent
To look upon when I else had fainted
In burning deserts, while you sipp'd ices
And snowy sherbets, and roam'd unfetter'd,
Is a deadly asp in the fruit and flowers
That you in your bitterness now bring to me;
But its fangs unfasten and it glides down from me,
From a Cleopatra of cold white marble.

I have but done what I would do over,
Did I find one worthy of so much devotion;
And, standing here with my clean hands folded
Above a bosom whose crime is courage,
The only regret that my heart discovers
Is that I should do and have dared so greatly
For the love of one who deserved so little.
And as for my lips' and my limbs' pollution,
They are purer than any strong man's new-wedded,
Stain'd without purpose in his coarse brute-passion.

Nay, say no more, nor attempt to approach me;
This ten-feet line lying now between us
Shall never be less while the land has measure.

See! night is forgetting the east in the heavens;
The birds pipe shrill and the beasts howl answer;
The red sun reaches his arms from the ocean,
And the dusk and the dawn kiss hands good-by,
But not for ever, as do you and I.

THE TALE OF THE TALL ALCALDE.

Shadows that shroud the to-morrow,
  Glists from the life that's within,
Traces of pain and of sorrow,
  And maybe a trace of sin,
Reachings for God in the darkness,
  And for — what should have been.

Stains from the gall and the wormwood,
  Memories bitter like myrrh,
A sad, brown face in a fir-wood,
  Blotches of heart's blood here,
But never the sound of a wailing,
  Never the sign of a tear.

THE TALE OF THE TALL ALCALDE.

> Thou Italy of the Occident!
> Land of flowers and summer climes,
> Of holy priests and horrid crimes;
> Land of the cactus and sweet cocoa;
> Richer than all the Orient
> In gold and glory, in want and woe,
> In self-denial, in days misspent,
> In truth and treason, in good and guilt,
> In ivied ruins and altars low,
> In batter'd walls and blood misspilt;
> Glorious, gory Mexico!

WHERE mountains repose in their blueness,
    Where the sun first lands in his newness,
And marshals his beams and his lances,
Ere down to the vale he advances
With visor erect, and rides swiftly
On the terrible night in his way,
And slays him, and, daring and deftly,
Hews from him the beautiful day
With his flashing sword of silver, —
Lay nestled the town of Renalda,
Far known for its famous Alcalde,
The judge of the mountain mine,
With a heart like the heart of woman,

And humanity more than human;
And famed for its maids and silver,
Rich mines and its mountain wine.

And the royalest feast of the year was given,
The yearly feast in commemoration
Of the Holy Mary's Annunciation;
And the ears of night were rent and riven
By turbulent men made stormy with wine —
Wine by virgins press'd from the vine,
Wine like gold from the San Diego,
Wine blood-red from the Saint Bennetto,
White and yellow and ruddy-red wine.
And the feast was full, and the guests afire,
For the shaven priest and the portly squire,
The solemn judge and the smiling dandy,
The duke and the don and the commandanté,
All sat, and shouted or sang divine,
Sailing in one great sea of wine;
And, roused, red-crested knight Chanticleer
Answer'd and echo'd their song and cheer.

They boasted of broil, encounter, and battle,
They boasted of maidens most cleverly won,

Boasted of duels most valiantly done,
Of leagues of land and of herds of cattle,
These men at the feast up in fair Renalda.
All boasted but one, the calm Alcalde,
Who sat stone-still in the wild wassàil,
Though hard they press'd from first of the feast,
Press'd commandanté, press'd poet and priest,
To tell, as the others, his own life's tale;
And steadily still the attorney press'd,
With lifted glass and his face aglow,
Heedless of host and careless of guest —
"A tale! the tale of your life, so ho!
For not one man in all Mexico
Can trace your history a half decade."
A hand on the rude one's lips was laid:
"Sacred, my son," a priest went on,
"Sacred the secrets of every one,
Inviolate as an altar-stone.
But what in the life of one who must
Have been so pure to be so just,
Have lived a life that is half divine —
What can there be, O advocate,
In the life of one so desolate
Of luck with matron, or love with maid,

Midnight revel or escapade,
To stir the wonder of men at wine?
But should the Alcalde choose, you know,"—
(And here his voice fell soft and low
As he set his wine-horn in its place,
And look'd in the judge's care-worn face) —
" To weave us a tale that points a moral,
Out of his vivid imagination,
Of lass or of love, or lovers' quarrel,
Naught of his fame or name or station
Shall lose in lustre by its relation."

Softly the judge set down his horn,
Kindly look'd on the priests all shorn,
And gazed in the eyes of the advocate
With a touch of pity, but none of hate;
Then look'd down into the brimming horn,
Half defiant and half forlorn.

Was it a tear? Was it a sigh?
Was it a glance of the priest's black eye?
Or was it the drunken revel-cry
That smote the rock of his frozen heart
And forced his pallid lips apart?

Or was it the weakness like to woman
Yearning for sympathy
Through the dark years,
Spurning the secrecy,
Burning for tears,
Proving him human, —
As he said to the men of the silver mine,
With their eyes held up as to one divine,
With his eyes held down to his untouch'd wine:

"It might have been where moonbeams kneel
At night beside some rugged steep;
It might have been where breakers reel,
Or mild waves cradle men to sleep;
It might have been in peaceful life,
Or mad tumult and storm and strife,
I drew my breath; it matters not.
A silver'd head, a sweetest cot,
A sea of tamarack and pine,
A peaceful stream, a balmy clime,
A cloudless sky, a sister's smile,
A mother's love, that sturdy time
Has strengthened as he strengthens wine,
Are mine, are with me all the while,

Are hung in memory's sounding halls,
Are graven on her glowing walls.
But rage, nor rack, nor wrath of man,
Nor prayer of priest, nor price, nor ban
Can wring from me their place or name,
Or why, or when, or whence I came;
Or why I left that childhood home,
A child of form yet old of soul,
And sought the wilds where tempests roll
Round mountains white as driven foam.

"Mistaken and misunderstood,
My hot magnetic heart sought round
And craved of all the souls I knew
But one responsive throb or touch,
Or thrill that flashes through and through —
Deem you that I demanded much? —
Not one congenial soul was found.
I sought a deeper wild and wood,
A girlish form and a childish face,
A wild waif drifting from place to place.

"Oh for the skies of rolling blue,
The balmy hours when lovers woo,

When the moon is doubled as in desire,
The dreamy call of the cockatoo
From the orange snow in his crest of fire,
Like vespers calling the soul to bliss
In the blessed love of the life above,
Ere it has taken the stains of this!

"The world afar, yet at my feet,
Went steadily and sternly on;
I almost fancied I could meet
The crush and bustle of the street,
When from the mountain I look'd down.
And deep down in the cañon's mouth
The long-tom ran and pick-axe rang,
And pack-trains coming from the south
Were stringing round the mountain high
In long gray lines, as wild geese fly,
While mul'teers shouted hoarse and high,
And dusty, dusky mul'teers sang —
'Señora with the liquid eye!
No floods can ever quench the flame,
Or frozen snows my passion tame,
Jouaña with the coal-black eye!
O señorita, bido a bye!'

"Environ'd by a mountain wall,
So fierce, so terrible and tall,
It never yet had been defiled
By track or trail, save by the wild
Free children of the wildest wood —
A wood that roll'd a sullen flood,
A sea that broke in snowy foam
Where everlasting glaciers rest,
Where stars and tempests have a home,
And clouds are curl'd in mad unrest
And whirl'd and swirl'd by crag and crest, —
An unkiss'd virgin at my feet,
Lay my pure, hallow'd, dreamy vale,
Where breathed the essence of my tale —
Lone dimple in the mountain's face,
Lone Eden in a boundless waste —
It lay so beautiful! so sweet!

"There in the sun's decline I stood
By God's form wrought in pink and pearl,
My peerless, dark-eyed Indian girl;
And gazed out from a fringe of wood,
With full-fed soul and feasting eyes,
Upon an earthly paradise.

TALL ALCALDE.

Inclining to the south it lay,
And long leagues southward roll'd away,
Until the sable-feather'd pines
And tangled boughs and amorous vines
Closed like besiegers on the scene,
The while the stream that intertwined
Had barely room to flow between.
It was unlike all other streams,
Save those seen in sweet summer dreams;
For sleeping in its bed of snow
Nor rock nor stone was ever known,
But only shining, shifting sands,
For ever sifted by unseen hands.
It curved, it bent like Indian bow,
And like an arrow darted through,
Yet utter'd not a sound nor breath,
Nor broke a ripple from the start;
It was as swift, as still as death,
Yet was so clear, so pure, so sweet,
It wound its way into your heart
As through the grasses at your feet.

" Once, through the tall untangled grass,
I saw two black bears careless pass,
And in the twilight turn to play;

I caught my rifle to my face,
She chid me with a quiet grace
And said, 'Not so, for us the day,
The night belongs to such as they.'

"And then from out the shadow'd wood
The antler'd deer came stalking down
In half a shot of where I stood;
Then stopp'd and stamp'd impatiently,
Then shook his head and antlers high,
And then his keen horns backward threw
Upon his shoulders broad and brown,
And thrust his muzzle in the air,
Snuff'd proudly; then a blast he blew
As if to say, No danger here.
And then from out the sable wood
His mate and two sweet dappled fawns
Stole forth, and by the monarch stood,
She timid, while the little ones
Would start like aspens in a gale.
Then he, as if to reassure
The timid, trembling, and demure,
Again his antlers backward threw,
Again a blast defiant blew,
Then led them proudly down the vale.

"I watch'd the forms of darkness come
Slow stealing from their sylvan home,
And pierce the sunlight drooping low
And weary, as if loath to go.
He stain'd the lances as he bled,
And, bleeding and pursued, he fled
Across the vale into the wood.
I saw the tall grass bend its head
Beneath the stately martial tread
Of the pursuer and pursued.

"'Behold the clouds,' Winnema said,
'All purple with the blood of day;
The night has conquer'd in the fray,
The shadows live, and light is dead.'

"She turn'd to Shasta gracefully,
Around whose hoar and mighty head
Still roll'd a sunset sea of red,
While troops of clouds a space below
Were drifting wearily and slow,
As seeking shelter for the night,
Like weary sea-birds in their flight;
Then curved her right arm gracefully
Above her brow, and bow'd her knee,

And chanted in an unknown tongue
Words sweeter than were ever sung.

"'And what means this?' I gently said.
'I spoke to God, the Yopitone,
Who dwells on yonder snowy throne,'
She softly said, with drooping head;
'I bow'd to God. He heard my prayer,
I felt his warm breath in my hair,
He heard me my desires tell,
And he is good, and all is well.'

"The dappled and the dimpled skies,
The timid stars, the tinted moon,
All smiled as sweet as sun at noon.
Her eyes were like the rabbit's eyes,
Her mien, her manner, just as mild,
And, though a savage war-chief's child,
She would not harm the lowliest worm.
And though her beaded foot was firm,
And though her airy step was true,
She would not crush a drop of dew.

"Her love was deeper than the sea,
And stronger than the tidal rise,

And clung in all its strength to me.
A face like hers is never seen
This side the gates of paradise,
Save in some Indian-Summer scene,
And then none ever sees it twice —
Is seen but once, and seen no more,
Seen but to tempt the sceptic soul,
And show a sample of the whole
That Heaven has in store.

"You might have pluck'd beams from the
    moon,
Or torn the shadow from the pine
When on its dial track at noon,
But not have parted us an hour,
She was so wholly, truly mine.
And life was one unbroken dream
Of purest bliss and calm delight,
A flow'ry-shored untroubled stream
Of sun and song, of shade and bower,
A full-moon'd serenading night.

"Sweet melodies were in the air,
And tame birds caroll'd everywhere.

I listen'd to the lisping grove
And cooing pink-eyed turtle-dove,
And, loving with the holiest love,
Believing, with a grand belief,
That every thing beneath the skies
Was beautiful and born to love,
That man had but to love, believe,
And earth would be a paradise
As beautiful as that above,
My goddess, Beauty, I adored,
Devoutly, fervid, her alone ;
My Priestess, Love, unceasing pour'd
Pure incense on her altar-stone.

"I carved my name in coarse design
Once on a birch down by the way,
At which she gazed, as she would say,
'What does this say? What is this sign?'
And when I gayly said, 'Some day
Some one will come and read my name,
And I will live in song and fame,
As he who first found this sweet vale,
Entwined with many a mountain tale,
And they will give the place my name,'

She was most sad, and troubled much,
And look'd in silence far away;
Then started trembling from my touch,
And when she turn'd her face again,
I read unutterable pain.

"At last she answer'd through her tears,
'Ah! yes; this, too, fulfils my fears.
Yes, they will come — my race must go
As fades a vernal fall of snow;
And you be known, and I forgot
Like these brown leaves that rust and rot
Beneath my feet; and it is well:
I do not seek to thrust my name
On those who here, hereafter, dwell,
Because I have before them dwelt;
They too will have their tales to tell,
They too will ask their time and fame.

"'Yes, they will come, come even now:
The dim ghosts on yon mountain's brow,
Gray Fathers of my tribe and race,
Do beckon to us from their place,
And hurl red arrows through the air
At night, to bid our braves beware.

A foot-print by the clear McCloud,
Unlike aught ever seen before,
Is seen. The crash of rifles loud
Is heard along its farther shore.'

* * * * *

"What tall and tawny men were these,
As sombre, silent, as the trees
They moved among! and sad some way
With tempered sadness, ever they, —
Yet not with sorrow born of fear.
The shadow of their destinies
They saw approaching year by year,
And murmured not. They saw the sun
Go down; they saw the peaceful moon
Move on in silence to her rest,
And white streams winding to the west:
And thus they knew that oversoon,
Somehow, somewhere, for every one
Was rest beyond the setting sun.
They knew not, never dreamed, a doubt,
But turned to death as to a sleep,
And died with eager hands held out
To reaching hands beyond the deep, —

And died with choicest bow at hand,
And quiver full, and arrow drawn
For use, when sweet to-morrow's dawn
Should wake them in the Spirit Land.

"What wonder that I lingered there
With Nature's children! Could I part
With those that met me heart to heart,
And made me welcome, spoke me fair,
Were first of all that understood
My waywardness from others' ways,
My worship of the true and good,
And earnest love of Nature's God,
Now that their dark days gathered near,
And came calamity and fear?
O idle men of empty days,
Go court the mountains in the clouds,
And clashing thunder, and the shrouds
Of tempests, and eternal shocks,
And fast and pray as one of old
In earnestness, and ye shall hold
The mysteries; shall hold the rod
That passes seas, that smites the rocks
Where streams of melody and song

Shall run as white streams rush and flow
Down from the mountains' crests of snow,
Forever, to a thirsting throng.

"Between the white man and the red
There lies no neutral, half-way ground.
I heard afar the thunder sound
That soon should burst above my head,
And made my choice; I laid my plan,
And child-like chose the weaker side;
And ever have, and ever will,
While might is wrong and wrongs remain,
As careless of the world as I
Am careless of a cloudless sky.
With wayward and romantic joy
I gave my pledge like any boy,
But kept my promise like a man,
And lost; yet with the lesson still
Would gladly do the same again.

"'They come! they come! the pale-face come!'
The chieftain shouted where he stood
Sharp watching at the margin wood,
And gave the war-whoop's treble yell,

That like a knell on fair hearts fell
Far watching from their rocky home.

"No nodding plumes or banners fair
Unfurl'd or fretted through the air;
No screaming fife or rolling drum
Did challenge brave of soul to come:
But, silent, sinew-bows were strung,
And, sudden, heavy quivers hung,
And, swiftly, to the battle sprung
Tall painted braves with tufted hair,
Like death-black banners in the air.

"And long they fought, and firm and well;
And silent fought, and silent fell,
Save when they gave the fearful yell
Of death, defiance, or of hate.
But what were feather'd flints to fate?
And what were yells to seething lead?
And what the few and feeble feet
To troops that came with martial tread,
And stood by wood and hill and stream
As thick as people in a street,
As strange as spirits in a dream?

"From pine and poplar, here and there,
A cloud, a flash, a crash, a thud,
A warrior's garments roll'd in blood,
A yell that rent the mountain air
Of fierce defiance and despair,
Did tell who fell, and when and where.
Then tighter drew the coils around,
And closer grew the battle-ground,
And fewer feather'd arrows fell,
And fainter grew the battle yell,
Until upon the hill was heard
The short, sharp whistle of the bird.

"The calm, that cometh after all,
Look'd sweetly down at shut of day,
Where friend and foe commingled lay
Like leaves of forest as they fall.
Afar the sombre mountains frown'd,
Here tall pines wheel'd their shadows round
Like long, slim fingers of a hand
That sadly pointed out the dead.
Like some broad shield high overhead
The great white moon led on and on,
As leading to the better land.

TALL ALCALDE.

You might have heard the cricket's trill,
Or night-birds calling from the hill,
The place was so profoundly still.

" The mighty chief at last was down,
The broken breast of brass and pride!
The hair all dust, the brow a-frown,
And proud mute lips compress'd in hate
To foes, yet all content with fate;
While, circled round him thick, the foe
Had folded hands in dust, and died.
His tomahawk lay at his side,
All blood, beside his broken bow.
One arm stretch'd out as over-bold,
One hand half doubled hid in dust,
And clutch'd the earth, as if to hold
His hunting-grounds still in his trust.

" Here tall grass bow'd its tassel'd head
In dewy tears above the dead,
And there they lay in crooked fern,
That waved and wept above by turn;
And further on, by sombre trees,
They lay, wild heroes of wildest deeds,

In shrouds alone of weeping weeds,
Bound in a never-to-be-broken peace.

"Not one had falter'd, not one brave
Survived the fearful struggle, save
One — save I the renegade,
The red man's friend, and — they held me so
For this alone — the white man's foe.
And I sat bound, a stone on stone,
And waked and watched alone; alone
I looked on all, asleep or dead:
Watched dead and living undismay'd
Through gory hair with lifted head.

" They bore me bound for many a day
Through fen and wild, by foamy flood,
From my dear mountains far away,
Where an adobé prison stood
Beside a sultry, sullen town,
With iron eyes and stony frown;
And in a dark and narrow cell,
So hot it almost took my breath;
And seem'd but an outpost of hell,
They thrust me — as if I had been

A monster, in a monster's den.
I cried aloud, I courted death,
I call'd unto a strip of sky,
The only thing beyond my cell
That I could see; but no reply
Came but the echo of my breath.
I paced — how long I cannot tell —
My reason fail'd, I knew no more,
And swooning fell upon the floor.
Then months went on, till deep one night,
When long thin bars of lunar light
Lay shimmering along the floor,
My senses came to me once more.

"My eyes look'd full into her eyes —
Into her soul so true and tried.
I thought myself in paradise,
And wonder'd when she too had died.
And then I saw the stripèd light
That struggled past the prison bar,
And in an instant, at the sight,
My sinking soul fell just as far
As could a star loosed by a jar
From out the setting in the ring,

The purpled, semi-circled ring
That seems to circle us at night.

"She saw my senses had return'd,
Then swift to press my pallid face —
Then, as if spurn'd, she sudden turn'd
Her sweet face to the prison wall;
Her bosom rose, her hot tears fell
Fast, as drip moss-stones in a well,
And then, as if subduing all
In one strong struggle of the soul,
Be what they were of vows or fears,
With kisses and hot scalding tears,
There in that deadly, loathsome place,
She bathed my bleach'd and bloodless face.

"I was so weak I could not speak
Or press my pale lips to her cheek;
I only look'd my wish to share
The secret of her presence there.
Then looking through her falling hair,
Still sadder — so that face appears,
Seen through the tears and blood of years —
Than Pocahontas bathed in tears,

She press'd her finger to her lips,
More sweet than sweets the brown bee sips.
More sad than any grief untold,
More silent than the milk-white moon,
She turn'd away. I heard unfold
An iron door, and she was gone.

"At last, one midnight, I was free;
Again I felt the liquid air
Around my hot brow like a sea,
Sweet as my dear Madonna's prayer,
Or benedictions on the soul;
Pure air, which God gives free to all,
Again I breathed without control —
Pure air, that man would fain enthral;
God's air, which man hath seized and sold
Unto his fellow-man for gold.

"I bow'd down to the bended sky,
I toss'd my two thin hands on high,,
I call'd unto the crooked moon,
I shouted to the shining stars,
With breath and rapture uncontroll'd,
Like some wild school-boy loosed at noon,

Or comrade coming from the wars,
Hailing his companeers of old.

"Short time for shouting or delay, —
The cock is shrill, the east is gray,
Pursuit is made, I must away.
They cast me on a sinewy steed,
And bid me look to girth and guide —
A caution of but little need,
For I on Sacramento's plain,
When mounted warriors thunder'd by
And train'd their barbs to face or fly,
Once sprang upon the stoutest steed
That swept unmaster'd through the band,
Fierce and unbridled, wild and bare
As fabled wing'd steed of the air,
And, clutching to his tossing mane,
Swept onward like a hurricane,
And, guiding him with heel and hand,
Lay like a shadow to his side,
And hurl'd the lance at topmost speed
Beneath the arch'd neck of my steed,
And pierced the cactus targe that stood
An imaged foe against the wood,

And heard the shouts of savage pride.
I dash the iron in his side,
Swift as the shooting stars I ride;
I turn, I see, to my dismay,
A silent rider red as they;
I glance again — it is my bride,
My love, my life, rides at my side.

"By gulch and gorge and brake and all,
Swift as the shining meteors fall,
We fly, and never sound nor word
But ringing mustang-hoofs is heard,
And limbs of steel and lungs of steam
Could not be stronger than theirs seem.
Grandly as some joyous dream,
League on league, and hour on hour,
Far from keen pursuit, or power
Of sheriff or bailiff, high or low,
Into the bristling hills we go.

"Into the snowy-hair'd McCloud,
White as the foldings of a shroud;
We dash into the dashing stream,
We breast the tide, we drop the rein,

We clutch the streaming, tangled mane —
And yet the rider at my side
Has never look nor word replied.

"Out in its foam, its rush, its roar,
Breasting away to the farther shore;
Steadily, bravely, gain'd at last,
Gain'd, where never a dastard foe
Has dared to come, or friend to go.
Pursuit is baffled and danger pass'd.

"Under an oak whose wide arms were
Lifting aloft, as if in prayer,
Under an oak, where the shining moon
Like feather'd snow in a winter noon
Quiver'd, sifted, and drifted down
In spars and bars on her shoulders brown:
And yet she was as silent still
As black stones toppled from the hill —
Great basalt blocks that near us lay,
Deep nestled in the grass untrod
By aught save wild beasts of the wood —
Great, massive, squared, and chisell'd stone,
Like columns that had toppled down

From temple dome or tower crown,
Along some drifted, silent way
Of desolate and desert town
Built by the children of the sun.
And I in silence sat on one,
And she stood gazing far away
To where her childhood forests lay,
Still as the stone I sat upon.
And through the leaves the silver moon
Fell sifting down in silver bars
And play'd upon her raven hair,
And darted through like dimpled stars
That dance through all the night's sweet noon
To echoes of an unseen choir.

"I sought to catch her to my breast
And charm her from her silent mood;
She shrank as if a beam, a breath,
Then silently before me stood,
Still, coldly, as the kiss of death.
Her face was darker than a pall,
Her presence was so proudly tall,
I would have started from the stone
Where I sat gazing up at her,

As from a form to earth unknown,
Had I possess'd the power to stir.

"'O touch me not, no more, no more;
'Tis past, and my sweet dream is o'er.
Impure! Impure! Impure!' she cried,
In words as sweetly, weirdly wild
As mingling of a rippled tide,
And music on the waters spill'd.
'Pollution foul is on my limbs,
And poison lingers on my lips;
My red heart sickens, hot head swims,
I burn unto my finger-tips.
But you are free. Fly! Fly alone.
Yes, you will win another bride
In some far clime where naught is known
Of all that you have won or lost,
Or what your life this night has cost;
Will win you name, and place, and power,
And ne'er recall this face, this hour,
Save in some secret, deep regret,
Which I forgive and you'll forget.
Your destiny will lead you on
Where, open'd wide to welcome you,

TALL ALCALDE.

Rich, gushing hearts and bosoms are,
And snowy arms, more purely fair,
And breasts — who dare say breasts more true
When all this dear night's deeds are done?

"'They said you had deserted me,
Had rued you of your wood and wild.
I knew, I knew it could not be,
I trusted as a trusting child.
I cross'd the bristled mountain high
That curves its rough back to the sky,
I rode the white-maned mountain flood,
And track'd for weeks the trackless wood.
The good God led me, as before,
And brought me to your prison-door.

"'That madden'd call! that fever'd moan!
I heard you in the midnight call
My own name through the massive wall,
In my sweet mountain-tongue and tone —
And yet you call'd so feebly wild,
I near mistook you for a child.
The keeper with his clinking keys
I sought, implored upon my knees

That I might see you, feel your breath,
Your brow, or breathe you low replies
Of comfort in your lonely death.
His red face shone, his redder eyes
Were like the fire of the skies,
And all his face was as a fire,
As he said, "Yield to my desire."
Again I heard your feeble moan,
I cried, "And must he die alone?"
I cried unto a heart of stone.
Ah! why the hateful horrors tell?
Enough! I crept into your cell
Polluted, loathed, a wretched thing,
An ashen fruit, a poison'd spring.

"'I nursed you, lured you back to life,
And when you woke and call'd me wife
And love, with pale lips rife
With love and feeble loveliness,
I turn'd away, I hid my face,
In mad reproach and deep distress,
In dust down in that loathsome place.

"'And then I vow'd a solemn vow
That you should live, live and be free.

And you have lived — are free; and now
Too slow yon red sun comes to see
My life or death, or me again.
Oh the peril and the pain
I have endured! the dark stain
That I did take on my fair soul,
All, all to save you, make you free,
Are more than mortal can endure:
But fire makes the foulest pure.

"'Behold this finish'd funeral pyre,
All ready for the form and fire,
Which these, my own hands, did prepare
For this last night; then lay me there.
I would not hide me from my God
Beneath the cold and sullen sod,
And ever from the circled sun,
As if in shame for evil done,
But, wrapped in fiery, shining shroud,
Ascend to Him, a wreathing cloud.'

"She paused, she turn'd, she lean'd apace
Her glance and half-regretting face,
As if to yield herself to me;

And then she cried, 'It cannot be,
For I have vow'd a solemn vow,
And God help me to keep it now!'

"I sprang with arms extended wide
To catch her to my burning breast;
She caught a dagger from her side
And plunged it to its silver hilt
Into her hot and bursting heart,
And fell into my arms and died —
Died as my soul to hers was press'd,
Died as I held her to my breast,
Died without one word or moan,
And left me with my dead — alone.

"But why the dreary tale prolong?
And deem you I confess'd me wrong,
That I did bend a patient knee
To all the deep wrongs done to me?
That I, because the prison-mould
Was on my brow, and all its chill
Was in my heart as chill as night,
Till soul and body both were cold,
Did curb my free-born mountain will
And sacrifice my sense of right?

"No! no! and had they come that day
While I with hands and garments red
Stood by her pleading, gory clay,
The one lone watcher by my dead,
With cross-hilt dagger in my hand,
The every white lord of the land
Who wore a badge or claim'd command,
And offer'd me my life and all
Of titles, power, or of place,
I should have spat them in the face,
And spurn'd them every one.
I live as God gave me to live,
I see as God gave me to see.
'Tis not my nature to forgive,
Or cringe and plead, and bend the knee
To God or man in woe or weal,
In penitence I cannot feel.

"I do not question school nor creed
Of Christian, Protestant, or Priest;
I only know that creeds to me
Are but new names for mystery,
That God is good from east to east,
And more I do not know nor need

To know, to love my neighbor well.
I take their dogmas, as they tell,
Their pictures of their Godly good,
In garments thick with heathen blood;
Their heaven with its harps of gold,
Their horrid pictures of their hell,
Take hell and heaven undenied.
Yet were the two placed side by side,
Placed full before me for my choice,
As they are pictured, best and worst,
As they are peopled, tame and bold,
The canonized, and the accursed
Who dared to think, and thinking speak,
And speaking act, bold cheek to cheek,
I would in transports choose the first,
And enter hell with lifted voice.

"I laid my dead upon the pile,
And underneath the lisping oak
I watch'd the columns of dark smoke
Embrace her red lips, with a smile
Of frenzied fierceness. Then there came
A gleaming column of red flame,
That grew a grander monument

Above her nameless noble mould,
Than ever bronze or marble lent
To king or conqueror of old.

"It seized her in its hot embrace,
And leapt as if to reach the stars.
Then looking up I saw a face
So saintly and so sweetly fair,
So sad, so pitying, and so pure,
I nigh forgot the prison bars,
And for one instant, one alone,
I felt I could forgive, endure.

"I laid a circlet of white stone,
And left her ashes there alone.
But after many a white moon-wane
I sought that sacred ground again,
And saw the circle of white stone
With tall wild grasses overgrown.
I did expect, I know not why,
From out her sacred dust to find
Wild pinks and daisies blooming fair;
And when I did not find them there
I almost deem'd her God unkind,
Less careful of her dust than I.

"Then when the red shafts of the sun
Came tipping down to where I stood,
I hail'd them with a redder one,
A lifted dagger red with blood,
And vow'd to dedicate my breath
To vengeance, for disgrace and death.

*　　*　　*　　*　　*

"Go read the annals of the North,
And records there of many a wail,
Of marshalling and going forth
For missing sheriffs, and for men
Who fell, and none knew where nor when,—
Who disappear'd on mountain trail,
Or in some dense and narrow vale.
Go, traverse Trinity and Scott,
That curve their dark backs to the sun:
Go, court them all. Lo! have they not
The chronicles of my wild life?
My secrets on their lips of stone,
My archives built of human bone?
Go, cross their wilds as I have done,
From snowy crest to sleeping vales,

And you will find on every one
Enough to swell a thousand tales.

  * * * * *

"The soul cannot survive alone,
And hate will die, like other things;
I felt an ebbing in my rage,
I hunger'd for the sound of one,
Just one familiar word, —
Yearn'd but to hear my fellow speak,
Or sound of woman's mellow tone,
As beats the wild, imprison'd bird,
That long nor kind nor mate has heard,
With bleeding wings
And panting beak
Against its iron cage.

"I saw a low-roof'd rancho lie,
Far, far below, at set of sun,
Along the foot-hills crisp and dun —
A lone sweet star in lower sky;
Saw children sporting to and fro,
The busy housewife come and go,
And white cows come at her command,
And none look'd larger than my hand.

Then worn and torn, and tann'd and brown,
And heedless all, I hasten'd down;
A wanderer wandering long and late,
I stood before the rustic gate.

"Two little girls, with brown feet bare,
And tangled, tossing, yellow hair,
Play'd on the green, fantastic dress'd,
Around a great Newfoundland brute
That lay half-resting on his breast,
And with his red mouth open'd wide
Would make believe that he would bite,
As they assail'd him left and right,
And then sprang to the other side,
And fill'd with shouts the willing air.
Oh sweeter far than lyre or lute
To my then hot and thirsty heart,
And better self so wholly mute,
Were those sweet voices calling there.

"Though some sweet scenes my eyes have seen,
Some melody my soul has heard,
No song of any maid, or bird,
Or splendid wealth of tropic scene,

Or scene or song of anywhere,
Has my impulsive soul so stirr'd,
Or touch'd and thrill'd my every part,
Or fill'd me with such sweet delight,
As those young angels sporting there.

"The dog at sight of me arose,
And nobly stood, with lifted nose,
Afront the children, now so still,
And staring at me with a will.
'Come in, come in,' the rancher cried,
As here and there the housewife hied;
'Sit down, sit down, you travel late.
What news of politics or war?
And are you tired? Go you far?
And where you from? Be quick, my Kate,
This boy is sure in need of food.'
The little children close by stood,
And watch'd and gazed inquiringly,
Then came and climb'd upon my knee.

"'That there's my ma,' the eldest said,
And laugh'd and toss'd her pretty head;
And then, half bating of her joy,

'Have you a ma, you stranger boy? —
And there hangs Carlo on the wall
As large as life; that mother drew
With berry stains upon a shred
Of tattered tent; but hardly you
Would know the picture his at all,
For Carlo's black, and this is red.'
Again she laughed, and shook her head,
And showered curls all out of place;
Then sudden sad, she raised her face
To mine, and tenderly she said,
'Have you, like us, a pretty home?
Have you, like me, a dog and toy?
Where do you live, and whither roam?
And where's your pa, poor stranger boy?'

"It seem'd so sweetly out of place
Again to meet my fellow-man,
I gazed and gazed upon his face
As something I had never seen.
The melody of woman's voice
Fell on my ear as falls the rain
Upon the weary, waiting plain.
I heard, and drank and drank again,

As earth with crack'd lips drinks the rain,
In green to revel and rejoice.
I ate with thanks my frugal food,
The first return'd for many a day.
I had met kindness by the way!
I had at last encounter'd good!

"I sought my couch, but not to sleep;
New thoughts were coursing strong and deep
My wild impulsive passion-heart;
I could not rest, my heart was moved,
My iron will forgot its part,
And I wept like a child reproved.
Never was Christian more devout,
Never was lowlier heart than mine,
Never has pious Moslem yet,
When bearded Muezzin's holy shout
Has echoed afar from minaret,
Knelt lowlier down to saint or shrine,
Than knelt that penitent soul of mine.

"I lay and pictured me a life
Afar from cold reproach or stain,
Or annals dark of blood and strife,

From deadly perils or heart-pain;
And at the breaking of the morn
I swung my arms from off the horn,
And turned to other scenes and lands
With lighten'd heart and whiten'd hands.

" Where orange-blossoms never die,
Where red fruits ripen all the year
Beneath a sweet and balmy sky,
Far from my language or my land,
Reproach, regret, or shame or fear,
I came in hope, I wander'd here —
Yes, here; and this red, bony hand
That holds this glass of ruddy cheer — "

" 'Tis he!" hissed the crafty advocate.
He sprang to his feet, and hot with hate
He reached his hands, and he called aloud,
" 'Tis the renegade of the red McCloud!"

Then slow the Alcalde rose and spoke,
And the lightning flash'd from a cloud of hair,
" Hand me, touch me, him who dare!"
And his heavy glass on the board of oak

He smote with such savage and mighty stroke,
It ground to dust in his bony hand,
And heavy bottles did clink and tip
As if an earthquake were in the land.
He tower'd up, and in his ire
Seem'd taller than any church's spire.
He gazed a moment — and then, the while
An icy cold and defiant smile
Did curve his thin and his livid lip,
He turn'd on his heel, he strode through the hall
Grand as a god, so grandly tall,
And white and cold as a chisell'd stone.
He pass'd him out the adobé door
Into the night, and he pass'd alone,
And never was known nor heard of more.

KIT CARSON'S RIDE.

Room! Room to turn round in, to breathe and be free,
And to grow to be giant, to sail as at sea
With the speed of the wind on a steed with his mane
To the wind, without pathway or route or a rein.
Room! Room to be free where the white-bordered sea
Blows a kiss to a brother as boundless as he;
And to east and to west, to the north and the sun,
Blue skies and brown grasses are welded as one,
And the buffalo come like a cloud on the plain,
Pouring on like the tide of a storm-driven main,
And the lodge of the hunter to friend or to foe
Offers rest; and unquestioned you come or you go.
My plains of America! Seas of wild lands!
From a land in the seas in a raiment of foam,
That has reached to a stranger the welcome of home,
I turn to you, lean to you, lift you my hands.

LONDON, 1871.

KIT CARSON'S RIDE.

"RUN? Now you bet you; I rather guess so!
But he's blind as a badger. Whoa, Paché, boy,
whoa.
No, you wouldn't believe it to look at his eyes,
But he is, badger blind, and it happened this wise.

"We lay in the grasses and the sun-burnt clover
That spread on the ground like a great brown cover
Northward and southward, and west and away
To the Brazos, to where our lodges lay,
One broad and unbroken sea of brown,
Awaiting the curtains of night to come down
To cover us over and conceal our flight
With my brown bride, won from an Indian town
That lay in the rear the full ride of a night.

"We lounged in the grasses—her eyes were in mine,
And her hands on my knee, and her hair was as wine

KIT CARSON'S RIDE.

In its wealth and its flood, pouring on and all over
Her bosom wine-red, and pressed never by one;
And her touch was as warm as the tinge of the clover
Burnt brown as it reached to the kiss of the sun,
And her words were as low as the lute-throated dove,
And as laden with love as the heart when it beats
In its hot eager answer to earliest love,
Or the bee hurried home by its burthen of sweets.

"We lay low in the grass on the broad plain levels,
Old Revels and I, and my stolen brown bride;
And the heavens of blue and the harvest of brown
And beautiful clover were welded as one,
To the right and the left, in the light of the sun.
'Forty full miles if a foot to ride,
Forty full miles if a foot, and the devils
Of red Camanches are hot on the track
When once they strike it. Let the sun go down
Soon, very soon,' muttered bearded old Revels
As he peered at the sun, lying low on his back,
Holding fast to his lasso. Then he jerked at his steed
And he sprang to his feet, and glanced swiftly around,
And then dropped, as if shot, with his ear to the
    ground;

Then again to his feet, and to me, to my bride,
While his eyes were like fire, his face like a shroud,
His form like a king, and his beard like a cloud,
And his voice loud and shrill, as if blown from a reed, —
'Pull, pull in your lassos, and bridle to steed,
And speed you if ever for life you would speed,
And ride for your lives, for your lives you must ride!
For the plain is aflame, the prairie on fire,
And feet of wild horses hard flying before
I hear like a sea breaking high on the shore,
While the buffalo come like a surge of the sea,
Driven far by the flame, driving fast on us three
As a hurricane comes, crushing palms in his ire.'

"We drew in the lassos, seized saddle and rein,
Threw them on, sinched them on, sinched them over
    again,
And again drew the girth, cast aside the macheers,
Cut away tapidaros, loosed the sash from its fold,
Cast aside the catenas red-spangled with gold,
And gold-mounted Colt's, the companions of years,
Cast the silken serapes to the wind in a breath,
And so bared to the skin sprang all haste to the
    horse —

As bare as when born, as when new from the hand
Of God — without word, or one word of command.
Turned head to the Brazos in a red race with death,
Turned head to the Brazos with a breath in the hair
Blowing hot from a king leaving death in his course;
Turned head to the Brazos with a sound in the air
Like the rush of an army, and a flash in the eye
Of a red wall of fire reaching up to the sky,
Stretching fierce in pursuit of a black rolling sea
Rushing fast upon us, as the wind sweeping free
And afar from the desert blew hollow and hoarse.

"Not a word, not a wail from a lip was let fall,
Not a kiss from my bride, not a look nor low call
Of love-note or courage; but on o'er the plain
So steady and still, leaning low to the mane,
With the heel to the flank and the hand to the rein,
Rode we on, rode we three, rode we nose and gray nose,
Reaching long, breathing loud, as a creviced wind blows:
Yet we broke not a whisper, we breathed not a prayer,
There was work to be done, there was death in the air,
And the chance was as one to a thousand for all.

KIT CARSON'S RIDE.

"Gray nose to gray nose, and each steady mustang
Stretched neck and stretched nerve till the arid earth
    rang,
And the foam from the flank and the croup and the
    neck
Flew around like the spray on a storm-driven deck.
Twenty miles! . . . thirty miles! . . . a dim distant
    speck . . .
Then a long reaching line, and the Brazos in sight,
And I rose in my seat with a shout of delight.
I stood in my stirrup and looked to my right —
But Revels was gone; I glanced by my shoulder
And saw his horse stagger; I saw his head drooping
Hard down on his breast, and his naked breast stoop-
    ing
Low down to the mane, as so swifter and bolder
Ran reaching out for us the red-footed fire.
To right and to left the black buffalo came,
A terrible surf on a red sea of flame
Rushing on in the rear, reaching high, reaching higher,
And he rode neck to neck to a buffalo bull,
The monarch of millions, with shaggy mane full
Of smoke and of dust, and it shook with desire
Of battle, with rage and with bellowings loud

And unearthly, and up through its lowering cloud
Came the flash of his eyes like a half-hidden fire,
While his keen crooked horns, through the storm of his
    mane,
Like black lances lifted and lifted again;
And I looked but this once, for the fire licked through,
And he fell and was lost, as we rode two and two.

    "I looked to my left then — and nose, neck, and
        shoulder
Sank slowly, sank surely, till back to my thighs;
And up through the black blowing veil of her hair
Did beam full in mine her two marvellous eyes,
With a longing and love, yet a look of despair
And of pity for me, as she felt the smoke fold her,
And flames reaching far for her glorious hair.
Her sinking steed faltered, his eager ears fell
To and fro and unsteady, and all the neck's swell
Did subside and recede, and the nerves fall as dead.
Then she saw sturdy Paché still lorded his head,
With a look of delight; for nor courage nor bribe,
Nor naught but my bride, could have brought him
    to me.
For he was her father's, and at South Santafee

Had once won a whole herd, sweeping every thing
　　down
In a race where the world came to run for the crown.
And so when I won the true heart of my bride —
My neighbor's and deadliest enemy's child,
And child of the kingly war-chief of his tribe —
She brought me this steed to the border the night
She met Revels and me in her perilous flight
From the lodge of the chief to the North Brazos side;
And said, so half guessing of ill as she smiled,
As if jesting, that I, and I only, should ride
The fleet-footed Paché, so if kin should pursue
I should surely escape without other ado
Than to ride, without blood, to the North Brazos side,
And await her — and wait till the next hollow moon
Hung her horn in the palms, when surely and soon
And swift she would join me, and all would be well
Without bloodshed or word. And now as she fell
From the front, and went down in the ocean of fire,
The last that I saw was a look of delight
That I should escape — a love — a desire —
Yet never a word, not one look of appeal,
Lest I should reach hand, should stay hand or stay heel
One instant for her in my terrible flight.

"Then the rushing of fire around me and under,
And the howling of beasts and a sound as of thunder—
Beasts burning and blind and forced onward and over,
As the passionate flame reached around them, and wove her
Red hands in their hair, and kissed hot till they died—
Till they died with a wild and a desolate moan,
As a sea heart-broken on the hard brown stone . . .
And into the Brazos . . . I rode all alone—
All alone, save only a horse long-limbed,
And blind and bare and burnt to the skin.
Then just as the terrible sea came in
And tumbled its thousands hot into the tide,
Till the tide blocked up and the swift stream brimmed
In eddies, we struck on the opposite side.

* * * * * *

"Sell Paché— blind Paché? Now, mister, look here,
You have slept in my tent and partook of my cheer
Many days, many days, on this rugged frontier,
For the ways they were rough and Camanches were near;
But you'd better pack up, sir! That tent is too small
For us two after this! Has an old mountaineer,
Do you book-men believe, got no tum-tum at all?

Sell Paché! You buy him! A bag full of gold!
You show him! Tell of him the tale I have told!
Why, he bore me through fire, and is blind, and is old!
. . . Now pack up your papers, and get up and spin
To them cities you tell of . . . Blast you and your tin!"

BURNS AND BYRON.

Eld Druid oaks of Ayr!
Precepts! Poems! Pages!
Lessons! Leaves, and Volumes!
Arches! Pillars! Columns
In corridors of ages!
Grand patriarchal sages
Lifting palms in prayer!

The Druid beards are drifting
And shifting to and fro,
In gentle breezes lifting,
That bat-like come and go,
The while the moon is sifting
A sheen of shining snow
On all these blossoms lifting
Their blue eyes from below.

No, 'tis not phantoms walking
That you hear rustling there,
But bearded Druids talking,
And turning leaves in prayer.
No, not a night-bird singing,
Nor breeze the broad bough swinging,
But that bough holds a censer,
And swings it to and fro.
'Tis Sunday eve remember,
That's why they chant so low.

AYR, 1870.

BURNS AND BYRON.

NOTE.

The day before my departure for Europe last summer, a small party sailed out to the beautiful sea-front of Saucélito, lying in the great Bay of San Francisco, forever green in its crown of California laurel; and there the fairest hands of the youngest and fairest city of the New World wove a wreath of bay for the tomb of Byron. I brought it over the Rocky Mountains, and the seas, and placed it above the dust of the soldier-poet, as desired. The wreath hangs now on the dark and dusty wall of the church at Hucknall Tokard above the tattered coat-of-arms of the Byrons, and the small stained tablet placed there by the Poet's sister.

Having come directly from Dumfries, I am bound to say that the contrast between the tombs of the two immortal poets was at least remarkable.

But in my pilgrimage to places sacred to the memory of Burns, I found none equal in interest to Ayr, the Doon, and their environs; perhaps it was because these places witnessed his birth, and his hard life's battles.

I LINGER in the autumn noon,
   I listen to the partridge call,
I watch the yellow leaflets fall
And drift adown the dimpled Doon.
I lean me o'er the ivy-grown
Old brig, where Vandal tourists' tools

Have ribb'd out names that would be known,
Are known — known as a herd of fools.

Down Ailsa Craig the sun declines,
    With lances levell'd here and there —
The tinted thorns! the trailing vines!
    O braes of Doon! so fond, so fair!
So passing fair, so more than fond!
The Poet's place of birth beyond,
    Beyond the mellow bells of Ayr!

I hear the milk-maid's twilight song
Come bravely through the storm-bent oaks;
Beyond, the white surf's sullen strokes
    Beat in a chorus deep and strong;
I hear the sounding forge afar,
And rush and rumble of the car,
    The steady tinkle of the bell
Of lazy, laden, home-bound cows
That stop to bellow and to browse;
    I breathe the soft sea-wind as well,
And now would fain arouse, arise;
I count the red lights in the skies;
    I yield as to a fairy spell.

Heard ye the feet of flying horse?
Heard ye the bogles in the air
That clutch at Tam O'Shanter's mare,
　That flies this mossy brig across?

O Burns! where bid? where bide you now?
Where are you in this night's full noon,
Great master of the pen and plough?
Might you not on yon slanting beam
Of moonlight, kneeling to the Doon,
Descend once to this hallow'd stream?
Sure yon stars yield enough of light
For heaven to spare your face one night.

O Burns! another name for song,
Another name for passion — pride;
For love and poesy allied;
For strangely blended right and wrong.

I picture you as one who kneel'd
A stranger at his own hearthstone;
One knowing all, yet all unknown,

One seeing all, yet all conceal'd;
The fitful years you linger'd here,
A lease of peril and of pain;
And I am thankful yet again
The gods did love you, ploughman! peer!

In all your own and other lands,
I hear your touching songs of cheer;
The peasant and the lordly peer
Above your honor'd dust strike hands.

A touch of tenderness is shown
In this unselfish love of Ayr,
And it is well, you earn'd it fair;
For all unhelmeted, alone,
You proved a ploughman's honest claim
To battle in the lists of fame;
You earn'd it as a warrior earns
His laurels fighting for his land,
And died — it was your right to go.
O eloquence of silent woe!
The Master leaning reach'd a hand,
And whisper'd, "It is finish'd, Burns!"

O sad, sweet singer of a Spring!
Yours was a chill uncheerful May,
And you knew no full days of June;
You ran too swiftly up the way,
And wearied soon, so over-soon!
You sang in weariness and woe;
You falter'd, and God heard you sing,
Then touch'd your hand and led you so,
You found life's hill-top low, so low,
You cross'd its summit long ere noon.
Thus sooner than one would suppose
Some weary feet will find repose.

O cold and cruel Nottingham!
In disappointment and in tears,
Sad, lost, and lonely, here I am
To question, "Is this Nottingham,
Of which I dream'd for years and years?
I seek in vain for name or sign
Of him who made this mould a shrine,
A Mecca to the fair and fond
Beyond the seas, and still beyond.

Where white clouds crush their drooping wings
Against the snow-crown'd battlements,
And peaks that flash like silver tents;
Where Sacramento's fountain springs,
And proud Columbia frets his shore
Of sombre, boundless wood and wold,
And lifts his yellow sands of gold
In plaintive murmurs evermore;
Where snowy dimpled Tahoe smiles,
And where white breakers from the sea,
In solid phalanx knee to knee,
Surround the calm Pacific Isles,
Then run and reach unto the land
And spread their thin palms on the sand, —
Is he supreme — there understood:
The free can understand the free,
The brave and good the brave and good.

Yea, he did sin; who hath reveal'd
That he was more than man, or less?
Yet sinn'd no more, but less conceal'd
Than they who cloak'd their follies o'er,
And then cast stones in his distress.
He scorn'd to make the good seem more,

Or make the bitter sin seem less.
And so his very manliness
The seeds of persecution bore.

When all his fervid wayward love
Brought back no olive-branch or dove,
Or love or trust from any one,
Proud, all unpitied and alone
He lived to make himself unknown,
Disdaining love and yielding none.
Like some high-lifted sea-girt stone
That could not stoop, but all the days,
With proud brow turning to the breeze,
Felt seas blown from the south, and seas
Blown from the north, and many ways,
He stood — a solitary light
In stormy seas and settled night —
Then fell, but stirr'd the seas as far
As winds and waves and waters are.

The meek-eyed stars are cold and white
And steady, fix'd for all the years;
The comet burns the wings of night,
And dazzles elements and spheres,

Then dies in beauty and a blaze
Of light, blown far through other days.

The poet's passion, sense of pride,
His sentiment, the wooing throng
Of sweet temptations that betide
The wild and wayward child of song,
The world knows not: I lift a hand
To ye who know, who understand.

In men whom men condemn as ill
I find so much of goodness still,
In men whom men pronounce divine
I find so much of sin and blot,
I hesitate to draw a line
Between the two, where God has not.

* * * * *

In sad but beautiful decay
Gray Hucknall kneels into the dust,
And, cherishing her sacred trust,
Does blend her clay with lordly clay.

The ancient Abbey's breast is broad,
And stout her massive walls of stone;

But let him lie, repose alone
Ungather'd with the great of God,
In dust, by his fierce fellow-man.
Some one, some day, loud-voiced will speak
And say the broad breast was not broad,
The walls of stone were all too weak
To hold the proud dust, in their plan;
The hollow of God's great right hand
Receives it; let it rest with God.

No sign or cryptic stone or cross
Unto the passing world has said,
"He died, and we deplore his loss."
No sound of sandall'd pilgrim's tread
Disturbs the pilgrim's peaceful rest,
Or frets the proud impatient breast.
The bat flits through the broken pane,
The black swift swallow gathers moss,
And builds in peace above his head,
Then goes, then comes, and builds again.
And it is well; not otherwise
Would he, the grand sad singer, will.
The serene peace of paradise
He sought — 'tis his — the storm is still.

Secure in his eternal fame,
And blended pity and respect,
He does not feel the cold neglect,
And England does not fear the shame.

NOTTINGHAM, 1870.

MYRRH.

*Life knows no dead so beautiful
As is the white cold coffin'd past;
This I may love nor be betray'd:
The dead are faithful to the last.
I am not spouseless — I have wed
A memory — a life that's dead.*

MYRRH.

FAREWELL! for here the ways at last
    Divide — diverge, like delta'd Nile,
Which after desert dangers pass'd
Of many and many a thousand mile,
As constant as a column stone,
Seeks out the sea, divorced — alone.

And you and I have buried Love,
A red seal on the coffin's lid;
The clerk below, the Court above,
Pronounced it dead: the corpse is hid.
And I who never crossed your will
Consent . . . that you may have it still.

Farewell! a sad word easy said
And easy sung, I think, by some . . .
. . . I clutched my hands, I turned my head
In my endeavor, and was dumb;

And when I should have said, Farewell,
I only murmur'd, "This is hell."

What recks it now whose was the blame?
But call it mine; for better used
Am I to wrong and cold disdain,
Can better bear to be accused
Of all that wears the shape of shame,
Than have you bear one touch of blame.

I know yours was the lighter heart,
And yours the hope of grander meed;
Yet did I falter in my part?
But there is weakness in defeat,
And I had felt its iron stride
While your young feet were yet untried.

I set my face for power and place,
My soul is toned to sullenness,
My heart holds not one sign nor trace
Of love, or trust, or tenderness.
But you — your years of happiness
God knows I would not make them less.

MYRRH.

And yet it were a bootless strife;
Too soon and sudden up the way
I hurried in the spring of life,
And wearied ere the noon of day.
I did not reach — was it a crime
That my life knew no summer-time?

And you will come some summer eve,
When wheels the white moon on her track,
And hear the plaintive night-bird grieve,
And heed the crickets clad in black;
Alone — not far — a little spell,
And say, "Well, yes, he loved me well;"

And sigh, "Well, yes, I mind me now,
None were so bravely true as he;
And yet his love was tame somehow,
It was so truly true to me;
I wished his patient love had less
Of worship and of tenderness:

"I wish it still, for thus alone
There comes a keen reproach or pain,
A feeling I dislike to own;

MYRRH.

Half yearnings for his voice again,
Half longings for his earnest gaze,
To know him mine always — always."

* * * * *

I make no murmur: steady, calm,
Sphinx-like I gaze on days ahead.
No wooing word, no pressing palm,
No sealing love with lips seal-red,
No waiting for some dusk or dawn,
Or sacred hour . . . all are gone.

I go alone: no little hands
To lead me from forbidden ways,
No little voice in other lands
Shall cheer through all the weary days;
Yet these are yours, and that to me
Is much indeed . . . So let it be . . .

. . . A last look from my mountain wall . . .
I watch the red sun wed the sea
Beside your home . . . the tides will fall
And rise, but nevermore shall we
Stand hand in hand and watch them flow,
As we once stood . . . Christ! this is so!

MYRRH.

But, when the stately sea comes in
With measured tread and mouth afoam,
My darlings cry above the din,
And ask, "Has father yet come home?"
Then look into the peaceful sky,
And answer, gently, "By and by."

  * * * * *

One deep spring in a desert sand,
One mossed and mystic pyramid,
A lonely palm on either hand,
A fountain in a forest hid,
Are all my life has realized
Of all I cherish'd, all I prized:

Of all I dream'd in early youth
Of love by streams and love-lit ways,
While my heart held its type of truth
Through all the tropic golden days,
And I the oak, and you the vine,
Clung palm in palm through cloud or shine.

Some time when clouds hang overhead,
(What weary skies without one cloud!)
You may muse on this love that's dead,

Muse calm when not so young or proud,
And say, "At last it comes to me,
That none was ever true as he."

My sin was that I loved so much —
But I enlisted for the war,
Till we the deep-sea shore should touch,
Beyond Atlanta — near or far —
And truer soldier never yet
Bore shining sword or bayonet.

I did not blame you — do not blame.
The stormy elements of soul
That I did scorn to tone or tame,
Or bind down unto dull control
In full fierce youth, they all are yours,
With all their folly and their force.

God keep you pure, oh, very pure,
God give you grace to dare and do;
God give you courage to endure
The all He may demand of you,
Keep time-frosts from your raven hair,
And your young heart without a care.

MYRRH.

I make no murmur nor complain;
Above me are the stars and blue
Alluring far to grand refrain;
Before, the beautiful and true,
To love or hate, to win or lose;
Lo! I will now arise, and choose.

But should you sometime read a sign,
A name among the princely few,
In isles of song beyond the brine,
Then you will think a time, and you
Will turn and say, "He once was mine,
Was all my own; his smiles, his tears
Were mine — were mine for years and years."

Blue Mountains, Oregon, 1870.

EVEN SO.

*Sierras, and eternal tents
Of snow that flash o'er battlements
Of mountains! My land of the sun,
Am I not true? have I not done
All things for thine, for thee alone,
O sun-land, sea-land, thou mine own?
From other loves and other lands,
As true, perhaps, as strong of hands,
Have I not turned to thee and thine,
O sun-land of the palm and pine,
And sung thy scenes, surpassing skies,
Till Europe lifted up her face
And marvelled at thy matchless grace,
With eager and inquiring eyes?
Be my reward some little place
To pitch my tent, some tree and vine
Where I may sit above the sea,
And drink the sun as drinking wine,
And dream, or sing some songs of thee;
Or days to climb to Shasta's dome
Again, and be with gods at home,
Salute my mountains, — clouded Hood,
Saint Helens in its sea of wood, —
Where sweeps the Oregon, and where
White storms are in the feathered fir.*

ATHENS, 1870.

EVEN SO.

SHE was not full tall, was not fairer than others,
　　But there was in her eyes, so proud and glorious,
A dream, a wonder, a dangerous witchery;
And when into yours they did look steadfastly
With a longing and trust as if asking sympathy,
As in talk, low-voiced, with your soul in confidence,
While her rich full lips, red-pouting and luscious,
Kept forth sweet-blended their mirth and sentiment,
A battery shelter'd by a brown flood of tresses,
That lay or lifted in the warm winds fretted
About a brow of most marvellous beauty—
You were less of a man than I should desire
To know much of, to have been unmoved.

　Where pine-tops toss curly clouds to heaven
And shake them far like to downs of thistle,
In a rift of cañon cleft so asunder
That it seem'd as 'twere earth's lips half open'd
Where men wrought gold from the rock-ribb'd moun-
　　tain,

She patient abode with her faithful mother.
And brawny giants, men brown'd and bearded,
Did bless the brown earth as she walk'd upon it,
And call her more pure than their yellow gold treasures.

By the trails sometimes that wound round the mountain
Above brave men toiling long at the sluices,
The cheery girl passing would kind and playful
Call to them all kind words of encouragement,
Then awake the echoes of the frowning mountains
With gushing laugh at their honest answers,
And pass then on in a blaze of glory.
They, blessing her heart, would then put from them
Their coarser thoughts, and, bent to the boulders,
Would recall fair faces far over the water,
And be, for her, the happier and better
For many and many a day thereafter.

In the shadows a-west of the sunset mountains,
Where old-time giants had dwelt and peopled,
And built up cities and castled battlements,
And rear'd up pillars that pierced the heavens,
A poet dwelt, of the book of Nature —

EVEN SO.

An ardent lover of the pure and beautiful,
Devoutest lover of the true and beautiful,
Profoundest lover of the grand and beautiful —
With a heart all impulse, intensest passion,
Who believed in love as in God Eternal —
A dream while the waken'd world went over,
An Indian summer of the sullen seasons;
And he sang wild songs like the wind in cedars,
Was tempest-toss'd as the pines, yet ever
As fix'd in truth as they in the mountains.

He had heard her name as one hears of a princess,
Her glory had come unto him in stories;
From afar he had look'd as entranced upon her;
He gave her name to the wind in measures,
And he heard her name in the deep-voiced cedars,
And afar in the winds rolling on like the billows.
Her name in the name of another for ever
Gave all his numbers their grandest strophes;
He enshrined her image in his heart's high temple,
And saint-like held her, too sacred for mortal.

* * * * * *

He came to fall like a king of the forest
Caught in the strong stormy arms of the wrestler;

EVEN SO.

Forgetting his songs, his crags and his mountains,
And nearly his God, in his wild deep passion;
And when he had won her and turn'd him homeward,
With the holiest pledges love gives its lover,
The mountain route was as strewn with roses.
Can a high love then be a thing unholy,
To make us better and bless'd supremely?
The day was fix'd for the feast and nuptials;
He crazed with impatience at the tardy hours;
He flew in the face of old Time as a tyrant:
He had fought the days that stood still between them,
One by one, as you fight with a foeman,
Had they been animate and sensate beings.

At last then the hour came coldly forward.
When Mars was trailing his lance on the mountains
He rein'd his steed and look'd down in the cañon
To where she dwelt, with a heart of fire;
He kiss'd his hand to the smoke slow curling,
Then bow'd his head in devoutest blessing.
His spotted courser did plunge and fret him
Beneath his gay and silk-fringed caroña,
And toss his neck in a black mane banner'd;

Then all afoam, plunging iron-footed,
Dash'd him adown with a wild impatience.

A coldness met him, like the breath of a cavern,
As he joyously hasten'd across the threshold.
She came, and coldly she spoke and scornful,
In answer to warm and impulsive passion.
All things did array them in shapes most hateful,
And life did seem but a jest intolerable.
He dared to question her why this estrangement:
She spoke with a strange and stiff indifference,
And bade him go on all alone life's journey.

Stern then and tall he did stand up before her,
And gaze dark-brow'd through the low narrow casement
For a time, as if warring in thought with a passion;
Then, crushing hard down the hot welling bitterness,
He folded his form in a sullen silentness
And turn'd for ever away from her presence:
Bearing his sorrow like some great burden,
Like a black night-mare in his hot heart muffled;
With his faith in the truth of woman all shatter'd
Like the shell of the cocoa dash'd to pieces
On the stones below from its stately bower.

He heard a laughter as if in mockery,
And, vaulting his saddle, he did take his journey
Through the densest wood by the darkest windings,
As the things best fitting his fate and humor,
And hurl'd a curse back over his shoulder.
Another had woo'd her, one gay, of earth earthy,
Another had won her, a gay dashing soldier —
With gold epaulets and a uniform polish'd,
With sword and red sash, and a tongue swift and ready
With loud talk of battles, of fine deeds of daring,
That wins so most willing the ear of all women,
He did win this jewel from the lordly mountain,
Of its wealth never counting, its worth never dreaming,
In truth not possessing one sense so accomplished
He could know its value had it all been told him.

* * * * * *

'Mid Theban pillars, where sang the Pindar,
Breathing the breath of the Grecian islands,
Breathing in spices and olive and myrtle,
Counting the caravans, curl'd and snowy,
Slow journeying over his head to Mecca
Or the high Christ-land of most holy memory,
Counting the clouds through the boughs above him,

That brush'd white marbles that time had chisell'd
And reared as tombs on the great dead city,
Letter'd with solemn but unread moral —
A poet rested in the red-hot summer.
He took no note of the things about him,
But dream'd and counted the clouds above him;
His soul was troubled, and his sad heart's Mecca
Was a miner's home far over the ocean,
Banner'd by pines that did brush the heavens.

When the sun went down on the bronzed Morea,
He read to himself from the lines of sorrow
That came as a wail from the one he worshipp'd,
Sent over the seas by an old companion:
They spoke no word of him, or remembrance.
And he was sad, for he felt forgotten,
And said: "In the leaves of her fair heart's album
She has cover'd my face with the face of another.
Let the great sea lift like a wall between us,
High-back'd, with his mane of white storms for ever —
I shall learn to love, I shall wed my sorrow,
I shall take as a spouse the days that are perish'd;
I shall dwell in a land where the march of genius
Made tracks in marble in the days of giants;

I shall sit in the ruins where sat the Marius,
Gray with the ghosts of the great departed."
And then he said in the solemn twilight . . .

"Strangely wooing are the worlds above us,
Strangely beautiful is the Faith of Islam,
Strangely sweet are the songs of Solomon,
Strangely tender are the teachings of Jesus,
Strangely cold is the sun on the mountains,
Strangely mellow is the moon in old ruins,
Strangely pleasant are the stolen waters,
Strangely simple and unwooing is virtue,
Strangely lighted is the North night-region,
Strangely strong are the streams in the ocean,
Strangely true are the tales of the Orient,
Strangely winning is a dark-eyed widow,
Strangely wayward are the ways of lovers,
But stranger than all are the ways of women."

His head on his hands and his hands on the marble,
Alone in the moonlight he slept in the ruins;
And a form was before him white-mantled in moonlight,
And bitter he said to the one he had worshipped:—

EVEN SO.

"Your hands in mine, your face, your eyes
Look level into mine, and mine
Are not abashed in anywise,
As eyes were in an elder syne.
Perhaps the pulse is colder now,
And blood comes tamer to the brow
Because of hot blood long ago . . .
Withdraw your hand? . . . Well, be it so,
And turn your bent head slow sidewise,
For recollections are as seas
That come and go in tides, and these
Are flood-tides filling to the eyes.

"How strange that you above the vale
And I below the mountain wall
Should walk and meet! . . . Why, you are pale! . . .
Strange meeting on the mountain fringe! . . .
. . . More strange we ever met at all! . . .
Tides come and go, we know their time;
The moon, we know her wane or prime:
But who knows how the fates may hinge?

"You stand before me here to-night,

EVEN SO.

But not beside me, not beside —
Are beautiful, but not a bride.
Some things I recollect aright,
Though full a dozen years are done
Since we two met one winter night —
Since I was crush'd as by a fall;
For I have watched and pray'd through all
The shining circles of the sun.

"I saw you where sad cedars wave;
I sought you in a dewy eve
When shining crickets trill and grieve:
You smiled, and I became a slave.
A slave! I worshipped you at night,
When all the blue field blossom'd red
With dewy roses overhead
In sweet and delicate delight.
I was devout. I knelt at night,
I knelt at noon, and tried to pray
To Him who doeth all things well.
I tried in vain to break the spell;
My prison'd soul refused to rise
And image saints in Paradise,

While one was here before my eyes.
You came between alway, alway.

"Some things are sooner marred than made.
The moon was white, the stars a-chill —
A frost fell on a soul that night,
And lips were whiter, colder still.
A soul was black that erst was white.
And you forget the place — the night!
Forget that aught was done or said —
Say this has pass'd a long decade —
Say not a single tear was shed —
Say you forget these little things!
Is not your recollection loath?
Well, little bees have bitter stings,
And I remember for us both.

"No, not a tear. Do men complain?
The outer wound will show a stain,
And we may shriek at idle pain;
But pierce the heart, and not a word,
Or wail, or sign, is seen or heard.

"I did not blame — I do not blame.
My wild heart turns to you the same,
Such as it is; but oh, its meed
Of faithfulness and trust and truth,
And gushing confidence of youth,
I caution you, is small indeed.

"I follow'd you, I worshipp'd you,
And I would follow, worship still;
But if I felt the blight and chill
Of frosts in my uncheerful spring,
And show it now in riper years
In answer to this love you bring —
In answer to this second love,
This wail of an unmated dove,
In cautious answer to your tears —
You, you know who taught me disdain.
But deem you I would deal you pain?
I joy to know your heart is light,
I journey glad to know it thus,
And could I dare to make it less?
Yours — you are day, but I am night.

"God knows I would descend to-day

Devoutly on my knees, and pray
Your way might be one path of peace
Through bending boughs and blossom'd trees,
And perfect bliss through roses fair;
But know you, back — one long decade —
How fervently, how fond I pray'd? —
What was the answer to that prayer?

"The tale is old, and often told
And lived by more than you suppose —
The fragrance of a summer rose
Press'd down beneath the stubborn lid,
When sun and song are hush'd and hid,
And summer days are gray and old.

"We parted so. Amid the bays
And peaceful palms and song and shade
Your cheerful feet in pleasure stray'd
Through all the swift and shining days.

"You made my way another way,
You bade it should not be with thine —
A fierce and cheerless route was mine:
But we have met, at last, to-day.

EVEN SO.

"You talk of tears — of bitter tears —
And tell of tyranny and wrong,
And I re-live some stinging jeers,
Back, far back, in the leaden years.
A lane without a turn is long,
I muse, and whistle a reply —
Then bite my lips to crush a sigh.

"You sympathize that I am sad,
I sigh for you that you complain,
I shake my yellow hair in vain,
I laugh with lips, but am not glad.

*　　*　　*　　*

. . . "His was a hot love of the hours,
And love and lover both are flown,
And you walk, like a ghost, alone.
He sipp'd your sunny lips, and he
Took all their honey: now the bee
Bends down the heads of other flowers,
And other lips lift up to kiss . . .
. . . I am not cruel, yet I find
A savage solace for the mind
And sweet delight in saying this . . .

EVEN SO.

Now you are silent, white, and you
Lift up your hands as making sign,
And your rich lips lie thin and blue
And ashen . . . and you writhe, and you
Breathe quick and tremble . . . is it true
The soul takes wounds, gives blood like wine?

*   *   *   *   *

. . . "No, not so lonely now — I love
A forest maiden: she is mine;
And on Sierras' slopes of pine,
The vines below, the snows above,
A solitary lodge is set
Within a fringe of watered firs;
And there my wigwam fires burn,
Fed by a round brown patient hand,
That small brown faithful hand of hers
That never rests till my return.
The yellow smoke is rising yet;
Tiptoe, and see it where you stand
Lift like a column from the land.

"There are no sea-gems in her hair,
No jewels fret her dimpled hands,
And half her bronzen limbs are bare:

But round brown arms have golden bands,
Broad, rich, and by her cunning hands
Cut from the yellow virgin ore,
And she does not desire more.
I wear the beaded wampum belt
That she has wove — the sable pelt
That she has fringed red threads around;
And in the morn, when men are not,
I wake the valley with the shot
That brings the brown deer to the ground.
And she beside the lodge at noon
Sings with the wind, while baby swings
In sea-shell cradle by the bough —
Sings low, so like the clover sings
With swarm of bees; I hear her now,
I see her sad face through the moon . . .
Such songs! — would earth had more of such!
She has not much to say, and she
Lifts never voice to question me
In aught I do . . . and that is much.
I love her for her patient trust,
And my love's fortyfold return —
A value I have not to learn
As you . . . at least, as many must . . .

EVEN SO.

   . . . "She is not over tall or fair;
Her breasts are curtained by her hair,
And sometimes, through the silken fringe,
I see her bosom's wealth, like wine,
Burst through in luscious ruddy tinge —
And all its wealth and worth are mine.
I know not that one drop of blood
Of prince or chief is in her veins:
I simply say that she is good,
And loves me with pure womanhood.
   . . . When that is said, why, what remains?

   . . . "You seem so most uncommon tall
Against the lonely ghostly moon,
That hurries homeward oversoon,
And hides behind you and the pines;
And your two hands hang cold and small,
And your two thin arms lie like vines,
Or winter moonbeams on a wall.
   . . . What if you be a weary ghost,
And I but dream, and dream I wake?
Then wake me not, and my mistake
Is not so bad: let's make the most
Of all we get, asleep, awake —

Take all we get with greedy cheek,
And waste not one sweet thing at all;
God knows that, at the best, life brings
The soul's share so exceeding small
That many mighty souls grow weak
And weary for some better things,
And hungered even unto death.
Laugh loud, be glad with ready breath,
For after all are joy and grief
Not merely matters of belief?
And what is certain, after all,
But death, delightful, patient death?
O cool and perfect peaceful sleep,
Without one tossing hand, or deep
Sad sigh and catching in of breath!

"Be satisfied. The price of breath
Is paid in toil. But knowledge is
Bought only with a weary care,
And wisdom means a world of pain . . .
Well, we have suffered, will again,
And we can work and wait and bear,
Strong in the certainty of bliss.
Death is delightful: after death

Breaks in the dawn of perfect day.
Let question he who will: the may
Throws fragrance far beyond the wall.
I pass no word with such: 'tis fit
To pity such: therefore I say
Be wise and make the best of it;
Content and strong against the fall.

"Death is delightful. Death is dawn,
The waking from a weary night
Of fevers unto truth and light.
Fame is not much, love is not much,
Yet what else is there worth the touch
Of lifted hands with dagger drawn?
So surely life is little worth:
Therefore I say, Look up; therefore
I say, One little star has more
Bright gold than all the earth of earth.

"Yet we must labor, plant to reap —
Life knows no folding up of hands —
Must plough the soul, as ploughing lands,
In furrows fashioned strong and deep.
Life has its lesson. Let us learn

The hard long lesson from the birth,
And be content; stand breast to breast,
And bear and battle till the rest.
Yet I look to yon stars, and say,
Thank Christ, ye are so far away
That when I win you I can turn
And look, and see no sign of earth.

* * * * *

. . . "You stand up so uncommon tall,
Your back against the falling moon,
And all your limbs are still, and all
Your raiment is as snow and stone.
What if I called you mine, my own?
What if I kissed you, mouth to mouth,
In all the passion of my South,
And should possess you oversoon?" . . .

He reached . . . he touched the marble stone:
He started up, he stood alone,
And up against the Grecian sky
White-marbled desolation stood.
The gaunt wolf hurried to the wood,
Within the wall, the owlet's cry

Was only heard; the silent blonde,
The brown wife with her babe at noon
That blessed him in the land beyond,
The mountain scene, the cedar trees,
The stormy and uncertain seas,
And all that he did see or seem
To see, had faded as a dream,
And fallen with the marble moon.

Cambridge: Stereotyped and Printed by John Wilson & Son.

DATE DUE